RAILWAYS AT THE TURN OF THE CENTURY, 1895–1905

Railways of the World in Color

RAILWAYS

AT THE TURN OF THE CENTURY

1895—1905

by

O. S. NOCK

Illustrated by

CLIFFORD and WENDY MEADWAY

THE MACMILLAN COMPANY

Library of Congress Catalog Card Number : 70763-02

First American Edition 1969
First published in Great Britain in 1969 by the
Blandford Press Ltd., London
The Macmillan Company

Printed in Great Britain

PREFACE

Following the publication of *British Steam Locomotives* and *Steam Railways of Britain*, we are now embarking on virtually a world-wide coverage, making marked periods in history rather than limitations of geography govern the scope of the contents. I need hardly add that this has greatly increased the task of both author and artists. While the colour schemes of British locomotives, carriages, and other items of both fixed and rolling-stock is fairly well documented over the years such is not the case with the majority of overseas railways. The official records simply do not contain information that is vital to the production of these books, and so we have had to seek out, in many countries far overseas, enthusiasts whose personal memories and notebooks could help to fill in some of the blanks. Even where models, paintings, and other evidence exists the colouring is not always reliable, and the research necessary in many cases has been lengthy and sometimes confusing.

One need hardly add, however, that the very difficulties that have beset our path have greatly increased the interest of the various searches, and made all the more exciting and rewarding the results actually attained. Numerous published works have been consulted, and a list of these is given in a bibliography at the end of this book, and I would like to express also my thanks to the Director of the Science Museum, London, and to the managements of the railway museums in Utrecht and Brussels. My warmest thanks are also due to the Archives Officer of the New South Wales Railways, Mr John H. Forsyth. Among individual friends who have helped greatly I must mention Baron G. Vuillet (Paris); Dr Giesl-Gieslingen (Vienna); Mr Frank Holland (Johannesburg); Mr Mortimer H. Clark (Gonluck, Victoria, Australia); Mr C. C. Singleton (Sydney); Mr W. W. Stewart (Auckland), and Mr Thomas T. Taber of New Jersey, U.S.A.

I am nevertheless very conscious of the fact that despite all efforts our coverage of the world scene at the turn of the century, and for a few years before and after, is not as comprehensive as I could have wished. Several important railways, several whole countries are missing. This is not by design but simply because reliable information has not reached us in time. In certain cases we have not yet established the local contacts who could find us the facts we need; but their researches have been protracted. The work of research is not ending with the publication of this book, and I hope that some more obvious gaps may be filled in later volumes of the series.

O. S. Nock

Silver Cedars,
High Bannerdown,
Batheaston,
Bath.

February 1969.

INTRODUCTION

The steam railway was a wholly British invention, and following the spectacular successes of the early railways at home it was no more than natural that British engineers should have been called upon to advise on, and actually to build, railways in many foreign lands. As the development of railways progressed, however, the engineers of France, Germany, Italy, Switzerland, and the U.S.A.—to mention only a few countries—developed practice to suit their own local conditions, while British railwaymen, ever conscious of the world scene, appreciated that some overseas ideas were worthy of adoption on the home railways.

Thus by the turn of the century railway practice, whether in locomotive or carriage design, in operating methods or in track construction began to partake of a synthesis of ideas, rather than remaining of an insular or strictly national nature. British practice had begun to incorporate certain Belgian and French features in locomotive design; American influence was evident in British carriage design, while British ideas had begun to influence Austrian locomotive practice. The detailed notes relating to the pictures contain numerous instances of good practices spreading far beyond the boundaries of national frontiers.

These points are interesting enough in themselves, but the world railway scene at the turn of the century, as portrayed in the 192 coloured illustrations, emphasizes a number of marked trends that are of the greatest interest. It is perhaps inevitable that the illustrations should contain a preponderance of locomotives. After all, the locomotive is essentially the centrepiece of the steam railway, and both in published literature and in the records of private individuals it has received far more attention than anything else. And quite apart from technicalities the pictures of locomotives can fairly speak for themselves at times.

One needs to turn no further among the coloured pictures than Nos. 15, 16, 17, and 18 to see four different varieties of the 4-4-0 type: the queer-looking French 'wind-cutter' of the Paris, Lyons, and Mediterranean; the elegant, highly ornate British designed Dutch State engine; the quietly dignified Caledonian 'Dunalastair' as purchased in its Scottish entirety by the Belgian Government, and the rakish, highly functional 'fast mail' engine of the Chicago and North Western. Some equally striking contrasts are to be found elsewhere in the book, where contemporary locomotives of diverse origins, and precepts are grouped together on facing pages. Elsewhere engines of a single country are displayed together, as in the case of Spain, where locomotives of British, French, and German origin were serving the same country.

In the countries of the British Commonwealth, it is natural to find locomotives of British tradition, and largely of British manufacture, predominating at the turn of the century. In India, for example, the railways were run almost entirely by men who had gone out from this country, and unconsciously perhaps the styles and practices of their 'parent' companies tended to permeate the individual Indian systems. The North Western, with its headquarters at Lahore, not only in its locomotive livery but in other respects tended to mould itself on the English London and North Western; the Great Indian Peninsula included some strong Great Western influences, though its locomotive livery was almost pure London–Brighton and South Coast. The East Indian had as locomotive engineer a very ardent disciple of Stroudley. English standards of safety in operation, and in signalling, were firmly established, adapted, and simplified where necessary to suit Indian conditions. It was natural that such circumstances should prevail throughout the existence of the British Indian Empire.

Further afield, there was greater independence of action, even by the turn of the century. In Australia, while British locomotives were generally preferred, there were several occasions when, in the face of urgent need for additional power and long delivery promises from the United Kingdom, locomotives of manufacturers' standard type were obtained from the U.S.A. This was no more than certain railways did in England at about the same time, when there was a remarkable upsurge in traffic. New engines were needed; the British locomotive building industry was committed to its maximum capacity and the Great Northern, the Midland, and the Great Central railways were compelled to purchase engines from the U.S.A. Some of these are illustrated in this book. The book also contains illustrations of American-built locomotives for India and South Africa at the same period. In New Zealand by the period of this book, the major influence in locomotive design had already become American rather than British, though on the efficiently managed railways in both North and South Islands a strongly independent policy was developed in every facet of railway working. There was no mere copying of ideas from elsewhere.

On the continent of Europe the scene was as fascinating as it was diverse. Most countries had a number of independent railways, and in Holland, Austria, and France, to mention only three, there were some railways owned by the State, and others privately. In Germany, although the once-independent states had been brought together politically under the imperial rule, from Berlin, the state railways were locally managed, and this book includes examples of the rolling-stock of Prussia, Baden, Saxony, and the Palatinate system, all very diverse in their appearance. In the technicalities of locomotive design it was the day of the compound in Continental Europe. In France, Germany, Austria, Switzerland, and Russia the various systems of compounding flourished, at a time when the nineteenth-century experiments with compounding in England were being abandoned and attention was being concentrated on improving the single-expansion type of locomotives. On the Continent, compounding was associated with a highly functional appearance of locomotives. Pipes, fittings, accessories were hung on outside, providing an appearance very untidy to British eyes. The contrast is heightened by the pictures grouped together in the later pages of this book.

This was largely the result of a different attitude towards locomotive management. The British attitude set considerable store on external neatness. Inside cylinders were generally favoured, working in conjunction with the Stephenson link motion, or Joy's radial gear. Technically, the inside cylinder engine gave a smoother ride, and created less racking stresses on the engine frame but our Continental friends preferred something in which the machinery was more 'get-at-able'. The various aids to efficiency and general accessories had to be outside. Furthermore, the finish of Continental locomotives was generally a great deal less ornate than was the customary in Great Britain. The outstanding exception was, of course, the Dutch State Railway, with its British-built 2-4-0s and 4-4-2s, so gaily adorned in bright green, with brown under-frames, and such a profusion of polished brass and copper work.

In presenting the locomotives and rolling-stock of the European countries in particular, in all their old individuality, one is to some extent turning over the pages of history, as one recalls the origin of the Dutch Rhenish Railway, and the intense competition for the Anglo-German mail traffic, which was then conveyed via Flushing. I can hear younger readers saying 'Flushing', where's 'Flushing?' and then following up the inquiry by asking what the English packet station was on this particular service. There was a time also when Dutch engines worked the Anglo-German mails as far into Germany as Wesel. Those were the days when all the famous Alpine routes were steam worked, and De Glehn compounds in pairs went slogging up the spirals to the St Gothard Tunnel, and Karl Gölsdorf was designing his epoch-marking compound 2-8-os for the Arlberg route. At that time the Simplon Tunnel did not exist, and the supremely picturesque Lötschberg route had not been built. The fast-running main line of the Swiss Jura–Simplon Railway terminated deep in the mountains at Brigue, from where in later years the Simplon Tunnel was driven.

Carriages provide a fascinating study in themselves, and in collecting a series of pictures from many parts of the world it is inevitably the unusual that have been chosen for illustration. Generally speaking the majority of carriages overseas were very plainly finished, both inside and out, and while some of the carriages included are not representative of the latest, or finest, a large amount of non-bogie stock of rather dingy appearance was included not only on internal services in European countries, but also on international trains. In America the large open saloon type of coach was almost universally favoured. Their high clerestory roofs made them spacious and airy inside, though the quality of the riding often left much to be desired. The long bogie coach to a large extent owed its origin to the quality of the permanent way on early American railways; it took more kindly to inequalities and the occasional weak spot in tracks spiked down direct on to the timbers. The majority of English railways were reluctant to adopt such long coaches, partly because existing sidings and other facilities would not accommodate them, and partly because of their greater dead-weight in relation to the number of passengers carried.

Another American feature that was in course of widespread adoption was the single central-coupler, as distinct from the British screw type, with side buffers and sometimes side chains in addition. In this country great store was set by having the couplings screwed tight, and when a locomotive was backing on to a train, or backing on additional coaches, care was taken to compress the spring buffers a little while the coupling up and screwing tight were in progress. Thus the coaches were tight together on the buffers throughout the train. If this was properly done there was a complete absence of jerk and shock when starting and stopping. This was a feature of British railway travel that all visitors were quick to appreciate. The American centre-couplers may have been very strong in themselves, but all too often there was a slight amount of slack after they were joined up, and sometimes there were very violent jerks when a train started.

This also happened on the British railways if the coupling up had not been done such as to have the buffers in contact. I once had two hours of apprehension on an express train running over the very hilly route between Carlisle and Edinburgh on which some covered vans had been attached next to the engines at Carlisle. Every time we started the jolt was so violent as to be almost frightening. It was not only most uncomfortable, but with a long and heavy train the sudden strain could easily have broken the couplings that were loose at the front end of the train. Although it is stepping rather outside our period, I may mention that modern British practice is to have the best of both worlds, in adopting the centre-coupler for its ease in coupling up, but at the same time retaining the side buffers. The adjustment of the centre-coupler is such that a slight compression of the side buffers is necessary to get the coupler to engage.

Perhaps the most English of all overseas railway carriages at the turn of the century were those of Australia, where the New South Wales and Victorian railways had to cater for an increasingly heavy suburban traffic from Sydney and Melbourne. New Zealand, while following the American style of bogie coach, developed a style entirely their own, which at one time included side corridors that were *open* at the sides. In India, as might be imagined, passenger rolling-stock exhibited a great diversity of accommodation, ranging from that provided on the mail trains for first-class passengers, and the humbler vehicles for native passengers. Distances were long and speeds were not high, and many journeys had to be made in the heat of the Indian noon-day. Accordingly, on all passenger stock, luxurious and humble alike, a curious form of awning, or sunshade, was fitted. While the amenities of travelling in cold weather were being increased by the introduction of steam heating, not a great deal had been done at that time to keep carriages cool in hot weather. In some dry and sandy districts one had perforce to have the windows open, and get covered in dust, or keep them closed and stifle! We include an interesting early example on the Great Indian Peninsula Railway where ventilation for summer conditions replaced the old sunshades.

Taking it all round, the turn of the century was an extremely interesting period on railways all over the world. Everywhere railways were then the pre-eminent means of travel by land, and while some administrations were still running the cheapest and least commodious carriages they could 'get away with', there was a marked trend towards greater luxury in travel on the more important routes. It was this trend more than any other that was causing the rapid increase in the size and power of locomotives, to haul heavier carriages. At this period speeds were on the increase in France and the U.S.A., and both countries for the first time in history were drawing level, if not slightly surpassing, the best achievements in Great Britain. The East Coast and West Coast routes from London to Scotland had won great renown in the race of 1895, when long stretches of both routes were covered at average speeds of 65 m.p.h., or more, from start to stop; but these were racing, rather than daily achievements, and an alarming accident at Preston in 1896 rather set public opinion against further acceleration for a time.

Nevertheless it was hard to subdue the Englishman's love of a sporting contest for long, and in 1904 a new race developed with inward-bound American mail traffic from Plymouth. On the North Atlantic Ocean the Blue Riband for the crossing from New York was then held by certain very fast German liners, and the railways serving Plymouth persuaded these steamship lines to set down their English passengers at Plymouth rather than Southampton, thereby saving nearly a day between New York and London. The London and South Western took the passengers and the Great Western the mails, and from each liner arrival at Plymouth there was a railway race to London. The climax was reached on 9 May 1904 when the Great Western mail train reached a speed of just over 100 m.p.h. in the descent of Wellington bank, near Taunton. So apprehensive however were the authorities that all who had participated were asked to keep the maximum speed a secret. Details were not published until several years later.

No such speeds were attained in ordinary daily travelling at that time. Anything above 75 m.p.h. was then unusual, and even in considerably later days the same standards of travelling persisted. I personally had been taking detailed notes of the running of express trains for nearly five years before I clocked a maximum of 80 m.p.h., and another ten years were to pass before I recorded my first '90'. Taking the world over at the turn of the century, it was only in Great Britain, France, and the U.S.A. that start-to-stop average speeds of 55 to 60 m.p.h. were scheduled. In most other countries maximum speeds were around 60 m.p.h. in Europe, and much less in most other continents. A few special Indian express and mail trains had spells at around 60 m.p.h., but on the narrow gauge lines, in Africa, for example, the general rate of travel was much slower.

ENGLAND

1 **London and North Western Railway**: a 'Teutonic' Class compound.

U.S.A.

2 **Webb Compound** supplied to the Pennsylvania Railroad.

3 **Eastern Railway of France**: a 'Crampton'.

4 **Paris–Orleans Railway**: 2–4–2 express engine.

5 **Northern Railway of France**: the 'Outrance' 4–4–0

6 **Paris, Lyons and Mediterranean Railway**: 'Henry' 2–4–2 express passenger engine.

PIONEER DESIGNS

U.S.A.

7 **Atlantic Coast Lines, U.S.A.**: the original 'Atlantic' engine.

ENGLAND

8 **The pioneer Smith compound**: No. 1619 North Eastern Railway.

BELGIUM

9 **Belgian State Railways**: modernised 2–4–0 express locomotive.

SOUTH AFRICA

10 **Cape Government Railway**: 4–4–0 express passenger locomotive.

HOLLAND

11 **Holland Railway**: Third-class corridor carriage.

GERMANY

12 **Prussian State Railways**: fourth-class carriage.

EGYPT

13 **Egyptian State Railways**: second-class carriage.

WALES

14 **Rhymney Railway**: bogie passenger carriage.

FRANCE

15 **Paris, Lyons and Mediterranean Railway**: 4-cylinder compound 4–4–0 locomotive.

HOLLAND

16 **Dutch State Railway**: 4–4–0 express passenger locomotive.

BELGIUM

17 **Belgian State Railways**: the Scottish-built 4–4–0.

U.S.A.

18 **Chicago and North Western Railroad**: the 'Fast Mail' 4–4–0.

19 **Midland Railway**: 'Princess of Wales' class 4–2–2.

20 **Glasgow and South Western Railway**: a Stirling 0–4–2 as running *circa* 1903.

21 **Great Western Railway**: rebuilt 2–4–0 passenger engine.

22 **Great Northern Railway**: American built 2–6–0 Mixed traffic engine.

U.S.A.

23 **Manhattan Elevated Railway, New York**: 0–4–4 tank engine.

ENGLAND

24 **Furness Railway**: a 'Cleator' class 0–6–2 tank engine.

ENGLAND (BUILT IN U.S.A.)

25 **Lynton and Barnstaple Railway**: narrow gauge 2–4–2 tank engine 'LYN'.

WALES

26 **Rhondda and Swansea Bay Railway**: 2–4–2 tank engine.

MALAYA

27 **Perak Government Railway**: 4–4–0 passenger engine of 1893 design.

MALAYA

28 **Sungei Ujong Railway**: 4–4–2 tank engine of 1899.

BURMA

29 **Burma Railways** 4–4–4 oil burning tank engine of 1899.

MALAYA

30 **Federated Malay States Railway**: the 'G' class 4–6–0 of 1899.

ENGLAND

31 **London–Brighton and South Coast Railway**: family saloon.

GERMANY

32 **Prussian State Railways**: mail van.

ENGLAND

33 **Great Eastern Railway**: milk van.

AUSTRIA

34 Austrian four-wheeled passenger carriage.

35 **Austrian State Railway**: 4–4–0 express passenger engine.

36 **Austrian State Railway**: Karl Gölsdorf's 2-cylinder compound 4–4–0.

37 **Austrian Southern Railway**: 4–4–0 express locomotive.

38 Mountain 0–8–0 for the Arlberg Route.

39 **Ballymena and Larne section, Belfast and Northern Counties Railway**: narrow gauge 2–4–2 compound tank engine.

40 **Listowel and Ballybunion Railwa** 'double' engine.

41 **Donegal Railways**: 4–4–4 type tank engine, *Hercules*.

42 **Londonderry and Lough Swilly Railway**: 4–6–2 tank engine.

43 **Swedish State Railways**: class 'Cc' 4–4–0 locomotive of 1900.

44 **Swedish State Railways**: class 'Kd' 0–6–0 goods locomotive of 1900.

45 **Swedish State Railways**: class 'Mb' iron ore 2–8–0 locomotive.

46 **Swedish State Railways**: class 'Ta' compound 4–6–0 locomotive.

LARGE TANK ENGINES

U.S.A.

47 **New York Central Railroad**: 2–6–6 tank engine.

ENGLAND

48 **Great Northern Railway**: 0–8–2 tank engine for London Underground traffic.

ENGLAND

49 **Great Eastern Railway**: the Decapod.

INDIA

50 **North Western Railway of India**: 2–8–2 tank engine.

CONTINENTAL EUROPEAN COMPOUNDS

FRANCE

51 **Northern Railway of France**: 4-cylinder compound express 4–4–0.

GERMANY

52 **Prussian State Railway**: 2-cylinder compound express 4–4–0.

SWITZERLAND

53 **Jura Simplon Railway**: 2-cylinder compound 4–4–0.

RUSSIA

54 **Vladikawska Railway, Russia:** 2-cylinder compound 4–6–0 express locomotive.

55 **Great Southern and Western Railway (Ireland)**: 4–4–0 express passenger engine.

56 **G.S. and W.R. (Ireland)**: a bogie brake-composite carriage.

57 **Midland Great Western Railway (Ireland)**: 4–4–0 express passenger engine.

58 **Midland Great Western Railway (Ireland)**: corridor carriage.

59 **East Indian Railway**: standard 4–4–0 express locomotive.

60 **Great Indian Peninsula Railway**: 4–4–0 express passenger and mail engine.

61 **Great Indian Peninsula Railway**: bogie brake-third carriage.

62 **Great Indian Peninsula Railway**: old style passenger brake van.

DISTINCTIVE COATS OF ARMS

CHINA

63 **Shanghai–Nanking Railway**: coat of arms.

INDIA

64 **Madras Railway:** coat of arms

IRELAND

Great Northern Railway (Ireland): coat of arms.

IRELAND

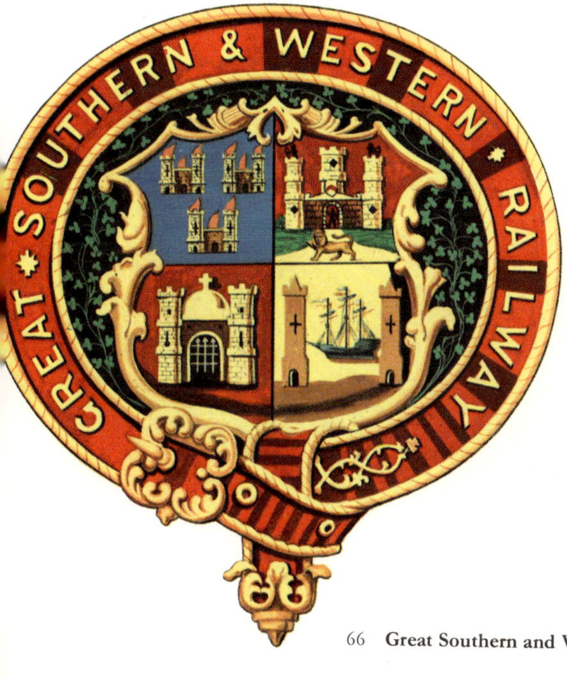

66 **Great Southern and Western Railway**: coat of arms.

67 **New South Wales Government Railways**: 'M40' class suburban tank engine.

68 **New South Wales Government Railways**: the celebrated 'P6' class 4–6–0.

69 **New South Wales Government Railways**: 'T.524' class 2–8–0 goods engine.

70 **N.S.W.G.R.**: second class non-corridor lavatory carriage.

71 **Great Southern Railway: of Spain** Scottish-built 2–6–0 engine of 1889–1905 period.

72 **Northern Railway of Spain**: 4–6–0 passenger engine of 1901–1903.

73 **Madrid, Zaragoza and Alicante Railway**: 4-cylinder compound 4–6–0.

74 **Andalusian Railway**: 4-cylinder compound 4–6–0.

CONTRASTS IN 4-4-0s

ENGLAND

75 **London and North Western Railway**: the 'Precursor'.

FRANCE

76 **Eastern Railway of France**: 4–4–0 non-compound express passenger locomotive.

SCOTLAND

77 **Caledonian Railway**: the Dunalastair IV class.

FRANCE

78 **Paris–Orleans Railway**: 4-cylinder de Glehn compound 4–4–0.

79 **Great Northern Railway (Ireland)**: 4–4–0 express passenger engine.

80 **Great Northern Railway (Ireland)**: composite semi-corridor carriage.

81 **Belfast and Northern Counties Railway**: 2-cylinder compound 4–4–0 locomotive.

82 **Belfast and Northern Counties Railway**: transporter truck, with narrow gauge carriage being conveyed.

83 **Canadian Pacific Railway**: 4–6–0 express locomotive.

84 **Canadian Pacific Railway**: observation car.

85 **Union Pacific Railroad**: 4–6–0 express passenger locomotive.

86 **Chicago and North Western Railroad**: 'Atlantic' type high speed 4–4–2 locomotive.

INDIA

87 **East Indian Railway**: standard 0–6–0 goods engine.

INDIA

88 **Nizam's Guaranteed State Railway, India**: 4–6–0 express locomotive.

FRANCE

89 **Paris–Orleans Railway**: 4–6–0 mixed traffic locomotive.

ENGLAND (BUILT IN U.S.A.)

90 **Midland Railway**: American built 2–6–0 goods engine.

91 **Wellington and Manawatu Railway, New Zealand**: 4–6–0 passenger engine of 1904.

92 **New Zealand Government Railways**: 41 ft. 'birdcage' saloon carriage.

93 **Wellington and Manawatu Railway**: 2–8–4 passenger tank engine.

94 **Wellington and Manawatu Railway**: 2–8–0 compound freight engine.

NORTH AMERICAN LOCOMOTIVE VARIETY

U.S.A.

95 **Big Four**: 'Atlantic' type express locomotive.

CANADA

96 **Canadian Northern Railway**: 4–6–0 passenger locomotive.

97 **Grand Trunk Railroad, Canada**: 4–6–0 passenger locomotive.

98 **Central Railroad of New Jersey**: 4–6–0 locomotive built 1902 ('Mother Hubbard').

ENGLAND

99 **Great Northern Railway**: the pioneer British 'Atlantic' engine.

U.S.A.

100 **Atlantic City Railroad**: Vauclain compound express 4–4–2.

FRANCE

101 **Northern Railway of France**: De Glehn compound 'Atlantic'.

ENGLAND (BUILT IN FRANCE)

102 **Great Western Railway**: De Glehn compound 4–4–2 No. 103, *President*.

STILL MORE ATLANTICS

FRANCE

103 **Paris–Orleans Railway**: De Glehn compound 'Atlantic'.

HOLLAND

104 **Dutch State Railway**: 'Atlantic' type express locomotive.

ENGLAND

105 **North Eastern Railway**: 'V' class Atlantic.

GERMANY

106 **Baden State Railways**: 4-cylinder compound 'Atlantic'.

107 **Shantung Railway, China**: 4–6–0 passenger locomotive.

108 **Shanghai–Nanking Railway**: 4–6–2 passenger tank engine.

109 **Shanghai–Nanking Railway**: 4–2–2 'Imperial Yellow' mail engine.

110 **Shanghai–Nanking Railway:** saloon carriage.

111 **Victorian Government Railways**: Clerestory roofed bogie composite carriage.

112 **Victorian Government Railways:** 4–4–0 express passenger engine 'New A' class.

113 **Victorian Government Railways:** 4–6–0 express passenger class 'Dd' of 1904.

114 **Victorian Government Railways:** passenger train guard's brake van.

115 **Great Indian Peninsula Railway**: 'Atlantic' type express locomotive.

116 **Bengal Nagpur Railway**: De Glehn 4-cylinder compound 'Atlantic'.

117 **East Indian Railway**: express passenger 'Atlantic' locomotive.

118 **North Western Railway of India**: standard 4–4–0 express locomotive.

119 **Central South African Railway**: 4–6–2 passenger engine.

120 **Central South African Railway**: 4–6–4 tank engine.

121 **Central South African Railway**: 2–8–2 freight locomotive.

122 **Z.A.S.M. (Transvaal)**: 0–6–4 main line tank engine.

SMALL TANK LOCOMOTIVES

FRANCE

123 **Western Railway of France**: 0–6–0 suburban tank engine.

HOLLAND

124 **Dutch State Railway**: 2–4–0 passenger tank engine.

ENGLAND

125 **Lancashire and Yorkshire Railway**: 2–4–2 tank of Aspinall design.

INDIA

126 **Great Indian Peninsula Railway**: 0–6–2 suburban tank engine.

127 **Austrian State Railways**: the Gölsdorf '170' class 2–8–0 of 1897.

128 **Vienna Metropolitan Railway**: Gölsdorf 2–6–2 compound tank engine.

129 **Austrian State Railways**: Gölsdorf 2–6–2 compound locomotive.

130 **Austrian State Railways**: Gölsdorf 4-cylinder compound 'Atlantic'.

131 **Norwegian State Railways**: 4–6–0 passenger engine.

132 **Danish State Railways**: 4–4–0 passenger engine.

133 **Danish State Railways**: 2–4–2 passenger tank engine.

134 **Swedish State Railways**: 2–6–0 type passenger engine.

SOUTH AMERICA

ARGENTINE

135 **Buenos Aires and Rosario Railway**: 2-cylinder compound 4–6–0.

ARGENTINE

136 **Buenos Aires Great Southern Railway**: 4-cylinder compound 4–6–0.

CHILE

137 **Antofagasta and Bolivian Railway**: 0–6–4 tank engine.

BOLIVIA

138 **Bolivian State Railway**: Fairlie type 'double' engine.

CONTRASTS IN STYLING

ENGLAND

139 **Great Northern Railway**: the Ivatt large-boilered 'Atlantic'.

GERMANY

140 **Palatinate Railway, Germany**: 'Atlantic' type express locomotive.

GERMANY

141 **Prussian State Railway**: a superheater 4–4–0 express locomotive.

GERMANY

142 **State Railway of Saxony**: a 2-cylinder compound 4–4–0.

EGYPTIAN STATE RAILWAYS

143 **Egyptian State Railways**: 2–2–2 express passenger locomotive.

144 **Egyptian State Railways**: 2–4–0 light tank engine, on extended loan.

145 **Egyptian State Railway**: 'Atlantic' type express locomotive.

146 **Egyptian State Railways**: 4–4–0 express locomotive.

ITALY

147 **Italian Southern Railway**: 4-cylinder compound 0–6–4 locomotive.

ITALY

148 **Italian Mediterranean Railway**: 2-cylinder compound 4–6–0.

ITALY

149 **Italian Mediterranean Railway**: 4–8–0 mixed traffic engine.

FRANCE

150 **Western Railway of France**: De Glehn compound 4–6–0.

CAPE

151 **Cape Government Railways**: 4–6–0 passenger and goods locomotive.

CAPE

152 **Cape Government Railway**: American built 'Atlantic' locomotive.

NATAL

153 **Natal Government Railway**: 4–10–2 main line passenger tank engine.

NATAL

154 **Natal Government Railways**: 4–8–2 standard tank engine.

ENGLAND

155 **Great Central Railway**: Pollitt 4–2–2 express locomotive for the London Extension.

INDIA (BUILT IN U.S.A.)

156 **Bombay, Baroda and Central India Railway**: American-built 4–4–0 express locomotive.

IRELAND

157 **Waterford, Limerick and Western Railway**: 0–6–0 goods engine.

U.S.A.

158 **Atchison, Topeka and Santa Fe Railroad**: 4–6–0 tandem compound express engine.

159 **New Zealand Government Railways**: 'Turtle-back' bogie passenger carriage of 1903.

160 **New Zealand Government Railways**: 'Wf' class 2–6–4 tank engine.

161 **New Zealand Government Railways**: 4–6–0 express passenger locomotive of 1898.

162 **New Zealand Government Railway**: Class 'UC' 4–6–0 passenger engine of 1901.

CARRIAGE DESIGN: INCREASING ELEGANCE

SOUTH AFRICA

163 **Central South African Railway**: main line bogie carriage.

BELGIUM

164 **Belgian State Railways**: second class bogie vestibuled carriage.

RUSSIA

165 **Moscow–Brest Railway**: restaurant car.

ENGLAND

166 **Midland Railway**: Pullman type sleeping carriage.

HOLLAND

167 **Dutch Rhenish Railway:** 4–4–0 express passenger locomotive, 'Rhine Bogie'.

HOLLAND

168 **North Brabant German Railway:** 4–6–0 express passenger locomotive.

169 **Belgian State Railways**: Belgian-built 'Dunalastair' type 4–4–0 locomotive.

170 **Belgian State Railways**: 4-cylinder 4–6–0 express locomotive.

SCOTLAND

171 **Caledonian Railway**: 30-ton mineral wagon.

INDIA

172 **East Indian Railway**: tank wagon.

173 **Barry Railway (South Wales):** mineral train brake van.

174 **Lynton and Barnstaple Railway:** open bogie goods wagon.

LARGE PASSENGER ENGINES

SCOTLAND

175 **Caledonian Railway**: McIntosh 4–6–0 express passenger engine No. 50.

SWITZERLAND

176 **Jura Simplon Railway, Switzerland**: express passenger 4–6–0.

PORTUGAL

177 **Minho-Douro Railway, Portugal**: 0–6–2 tender engine.

ENGLAND

178 **North Eastern Railway**: express passenger 4–6–0 class ‘S1’.

U.S.A.

179 **Wabash Railroad, U.S.A.**: open vestibuled car.

ENGLAND

180 **Cheshire Lines Committee**: 12-wheeled composite bogie carriage.

INDIA

181 **South Indian Railway**: bogie composite carriage.

IRELAND

182 **Dublin, Wicklow and Wexford Railway**: restaurant car for the Waterford Mail.

TURN OF THE CENTURY DEVELOPMENTS

ENGLAND

183 **Great Western Railway**: experimental 2–6–0 heavy freight engine ('Kruger').

U.S.A.

184 **Lake Shore and Michigan Southern**: 2–6–2 express passenger locomotive.

U.S.A.

185 **Pennsylvania Railroad**: class 'E1' 'Atlantic' of 1899.

FRANCE

186 **Paris, Lyons and Mediterranean Railway**: 4–6–0 mixed traffic locomotive.

FRANCE

187/188 A group of typical French mechanically worked signals.

ENGLAND

189 **London and South Western Railway**: Dugald Drummond's 4-cylinder 4–6–0 mixed traffic engine.

FRANCE

190 **Eastern Railway of France**: 4-cylinder compound 4–6–0 locomotive.

RUSSIA

191 A Russian 0–8–0 shunting tank engine.

SWITZERLAND

192 **Gotthard Railway**: 0–8–0 heavy freight locomotive.

RAILWAYS OF THE WORLD IN DETAIL

1 **London and North Western Railway:** A 'Teutonic' Class Compound.

Of all locomotives in service at the turn of the century none created a greater world-wide interest than the Webb compounds of the London and North Western Railway. Their inventor, Francis W. Webb, Chief Mechanical Engineer from 1871 to 1903, became a man of towering stature in the railway and engineering world, and the height of productivity and quality of finish achieved at Crewe Works were unsurpassed at the time. The three-cylinder engines of the 'Teutonic' class, although only ten in number, were the best of all the Webb compounds, and made a reputation for the punctual handling of heavy loads and an ability to run very fast when necessary. The *Jeanie Deans* of this class worked the afternoon Scottish corridor train from Euston to Crewe, returning with the corresponding southbound train with scarcely a break for 8½ years. The loads were usually about 300 tons, and the average speeds 50 m.p.h. The engine illustrated, the *Adriatic*, made the record run on the last night of the race to Aberdeen in 1895, covering the 158 miles from Euston to Crewe non-stop in 148 minutes, albeit with only a light load of 70 tons. Other engines of the class have been recorded at speeds up to 87 m.p.h., which was an unusual speed for the 'nineties' of the last century.

2 **Webb Compound:** supplied to the Pennsylvania Railroad.

Interest in the Webb compounds led to trials on various other railways. British law forbade the London and North Western Railway or any railway to build locomotives for other than its own use, and when the Pennsylvania wished to have a Webb compound for trial arrangements were made for the necessary drawings to be supplied from Crewe to Beyer, Peacock & Co. of Manchester. The engine in question was one of the earlier three-cylinder class known as the 'Dreadnoughts', and apart from smaller driving wheels they had the same design characteristics as the larger 'Teutonics'. There were two high pressure cylinders outside, driving the rear pair of wheels, and one very large low pressure cylinder driving the leading pair. The driving wheels were not coupled, and this curious feature gave certain difficulties in starting. The engine exported to the U.S.A. was fitted with a cow-catcher, and on arrival in America was later equipped with a much larger and commodious cab, and a typical bell. In our picture the engine is shown in the plain dark green style in use on the Pennsylvania in the early 1900s, though other contemporary locomotives had the characteristic polished boiler cladding in 'blued' steel. From all accounts the Webb compound was not liked on the Pennsylvania and no more were purchased from England.

3 **Eastern Railway of France:** A 'Crampton'.

The accompanying illustration, which was based on quite a recent photograph, shows what is probably the sole survivor of a very famous design of locomotive. It originated from the English engineer T. R. Crampton, and the first examples were supplied to Belgium in 1846. The Crampton type of locomotive, like some great 'stern-wheeler' paddle-steamer, never made much headway in England; but it was extensively used in France, particularly on the one-time Paris–Strasburg Railway, later the Chemin de Fer de l'Est. These picturesque engines were standard for the fastest express working on the Est main line from 1852 to 1878, and although they began to be displaced from the crack trains from the latter date they continued in service until well into the present century. The last of them, named *Le Continent*, was not withdrawn till July 1914. But the onset of war brought the reprieve, and throughout the war she did duty as a shunting engine. In 1925 she was restored and in 1931 enthroned on a pedestal at the Gare de l'Est, Paris. In recent years she has been restored to full working order and the photograph from which this illustration was prepared shows her in full steam hauling a train. *Le Continent* was one of the earliest of the standard type used on the Est, and was built in 1852.

4 **Paris–Orléans Railway:** 2-4-2 Express Engine.

Locomotives of this somewhat ancient appearance were still engaged in first-class express passenger work at the turn of the century. The Paris–Orléans Railway has an easily graded main line and the booked speeds were then not very high. Quite apart from the general look of antiquity these engines had some interesting design features, such as the Gooch type of valve gear and the valves arranged on a slope, as clearly seen in our picture. The boiler centre was pitched very low, and this gave the engines a stability in running. From the observations of those who have ridden on their footplates they were very comfortable at speed. They did not have to work very hard, even in the principal main line duties. A typical working was on the 1 p.m. express from Paris to the south booked to cover 74 miles from the Austerlitz station to Les Aubrais (Orléans) in 96 minutes. There were some curious restrictions of speed on that line. Some important trains were limited to a maximum speed of 62 m.p.h. while others were allowed to run at the legal maximum of $74\frac{1}{2}$ m.p.h. (120 km.p.h.). But the 1 p.m. needed no such haste, and the easy schedule could be kept without exceeding 52 or 53 m.p.h. Despite their antiquity, engines of this type were still in service up to the Second World War, and then called upon to run much faster on local trains than when they were on the main line.

5 **Northern Railway of France:** The 'Outrance' 4-4-0.

In 1866 Archibald Sturrock the famous Locomotive Superintendent of the English Great Northern Railway, designed some very large and powerful 2-4-0 express engines, with massive double frames throughout and a large boiler and firebox. They arrived from Fowler's works at Leeds just at the time when Patrick Stirling was taking over from Sturrock, and the former engineer favoured single-wheelers for express work. But while these big engines had a comparatively short stay on express work on the Great Northern Railway their design created a great impression in France, and one outcome was the production of a very similar design on the Northern Railway, later developed into a standard 4-4-0 class for the heaviest work. These Nord engines were as massively built as their English progenitors, and would stand any amount of hard thrashing. On the trains from Paris to the Channel ports with the English boat trains, and on the north-eastern main line to Arras and

Lille, and on the line that connected up with the Belgian railways these engines were often worked at their limit for hours: '*à la outrance*' and they became known as the 'Outrance' class!—in other words, 'the all-out engines'.

6 **Paris, Lyons and Mediterranean Railway:** 'Henry' 2-4-2 Express Passenger Engine.

As long ago as Victorian times English people were travelling to the French Riviera in winter to avoid the rigours of the home climate, and in making the long journey by train they travelled from Paris southwards over the tracks of the Paris, Lyons and Mediterranean Railway, passing Dijon, and the celebrated wine-producing districts of Burgundy, and at Lyons coming to the Valley of the Rhône. Over this long haul—536 miles from Paris to Marseilles alone, before turning eastwards along the Riviera coast—the quaint 2-4-2 engines of Monsieur Henry were in regular use. Travellers to the south usually going by night and facing all the rigours then experienced in such a journey would not be very interested in the type of locomotive used; but on the section along the Riviera coast one could hardly miss them. At Cannes and Menton the track ran close to the shore, while at Monte Carlo the line used to curve sharply round at the very foot of the world-famous casino. The heavier trains would be worked by a pair of these engines. The design dates from 1879, but they were still in regular express passenger service until well into the present century. They were not such fast or free runners as their counterparts on the Paris–Orléans; but for hard work with heavy trains of the day they were admirable.

7 **Atlantic Coast Lines, U.S.A.:** The Original 'Atlantic' Engine.

In 1894 the American firm of Burnham, Williams and Co., later world famous as the Baldwin Locomotive Company, produced the first-ever express passenger tender locomotive of the 4-4-2 type. There had been, six years earlier, a freak engine of the same wheel arrangement, but the Atlantic Coast example was the first of the orthodox type, and certainly the first to survive. The 4-4-2 type had the advantage over the 4-4-0 of permitting a large and wide firebox in the rear of the coupled wheels, and it was at once attractive to those railways which had to use inferior kinds of fuel. Because of the place of its origin, and the fame that its performance won, the 4-4-2 became known as the 'Atlantic' type. The design illustrated with two outside cylinders driving the rear pair of coupled wheels was the subject of a patent granted to William P. Henszey, a partner in the firm of Burnham, Williams and Co. This pioneer 'Atlantic' had cylinders 19 in. diameter by 24 in. stroke; coupled wheels 6 ft. diameter; a total heating surface of 2047 sq. ft.; a grate area of 26 sq. ft., and worked at a pressure of 180 lb. per sq. in. As described under ref. 99 the first British 'Atlantic', the Great Northern No. 990, was completed in 1898, and the similarity in many of the dimensions between that engine and the Atlantic Coast Lines of 1894 was quite striking.

8 **North Eastern Railway:** The Pioneer Smith Compound No. 1619.

The history of compound locomotives on the railways of the world is full of complexities and contradictions. Some systems of compounding tried on one railway and discarded have been widely adopted elsewhere, while others, such as the Webb, found little or no application outside their parent company. The system devised by W. M. Smith, Chief Locomotive Draughtsman of the North Eastern Railway, was one of the simplest and most successful of them all; and yet it was applied to only one locomotive on the North Eastern Railway. It was subsequently used to great advantage on the Midland and London, Midland and Scottish railways, and also to a limited extent on the Great Central and on the Great Northern of Ireland. Smith's three-cylinder system had one high pressure cylinder inside and two low pressure outside. It made for a strong, and simply constructed engine and the one North Eastern example, the 4-4-0 No. 1619 illustrated, which was built at Gateshead in 1898 was very successful. Smith obtained authority to extend the application by building two large Atlantic engines as four-cylinder compounds. These were equally successful but the Chief Mechanical Engineer preferred the three-cylinder simple system, instead of compounding, and no more Smith compounds were built. Engine No. 1619 stands as the true prototype of 240 three-cylinder compounds on the London, Midland, and Scottish Railway.

9 **Belgian State Railways:** Modernized 2-4-0 Express Locomotive.

In the latter part of the nineteenth century the locomotives of the Belgian State Railways presented some of the quaintest and most individual-looking of any in Europe. The engines carried the Continental practice of hanging every conceivable fitting outside to extremes, but included the added peculiarity of *square* funnels. The engine illustrated, however, shows one of the 2-4-0s of 1865–75 vintage as modernized around 1900, with a large diameter cylindro-conical chimney; a much neater general appearance, and the new brown livery, that superseded the older black with red livery. There is no doubt that the purchase of the five 'Dunalastair' 4-4-0s from Scotland (ref. 17) in 1898 greatly influenced Belgian practice, though not to the extent of copying the blue livery. Examples of many of the older Belgian locomotives are represented by magnificently constructed scale models in the railway museum in the Nord station at Brussels. These 2-4-0s had cylinders 17 in. diameter by 22 in. stroke; the coupled wheels were 6 ft. 7 in. diameter and steam distribution was by means of the Stephenson link motion.

10 **Cape Government Railway:** 4-4-0 Express Passenger Locomotive.

The standard railway gauge in South Africa is 3 ft. 6 in. and some locomotives of remarkable size and power have been put into service in recent years. At the period covered by this book the railways had, however, not yet been brought under a single administration, and in the Cape of Good Hope the Government railway, continuing its previous practice of purchasing locomotives from Great Britain, was just at the point of changing from the traditional 4-4-0s and 0-6-0s of the nineteenth century to much larger engines. The handsome outside-cylinder 4-4-0 shown in our picture was one of a batch supplied in 1903 by the North British Locomotive Co. Ltd, which firm had just been formed by the amalgamation of Neilson Reid, Dübs, and Sharp Stewart. Although a strong British affinity can be seen in the general appearance, and in the use of Stephenson link motion inside the frames, the large cab and the huge headlight will be noticed; also the small diameter bogie wheels. The headlight is a very necessary feature of equipment in South Africa, because in the open country the lines are unfenced, and wild animals that are of more attraction to the big-game hunter than the railwayman are apt to stray on the tracks at night.

11 **Holland Railway:** Third-class Corridor Carriage.

This railway, serving south Holland, had as its full title the Hollandsche Ijzerin Spoorveg Maatschappij, and used the rather curious form of carriage illustrated on a number of its secondary passenger services. These trains were themselves unusual in conveying only second- and third-class passengers, and the peculiar form of coach construction was designed to suit conditions at some of the stopping places. Otherwise it would be difficult to appreciate why valuable seating space was given up to provide a corridor from end to end. These trains not only stopped at all the intermediate stations but stopped when required at the watchposts situated at all important level-crossings. There were no platforms at these watchposts so steps were provided at the end platforms of the corridor carriages. Passengers entering or leaving at the watchposts climbed the steps to the end platform of the carriage and then made their way to the compartments. Although the windows were arranged in the conventional manner there were no doors to individual compartments except from the corridor. At the other end of the carriage there was another set of steps leading to the luggage compartments.

12 **Prussian State Railways:** Fourth-class Carriage.

As if travelling conditions were not spartan enough in the Continental 'thirds' of the nineteenth century, the various German State railways went one better—to be truthful one worse, albeit at still lower fares. The carriage illustrated is one of many on the Prussian State Railways. The interiors were plain and bare, with bench seats round the sides. Most of the passengers had to stand, though some brought their own seats in the form of primitive 'camp stools'. These carriages were evidently intended for mass transportation, and frequently carried sixty passengers or more. They were not confined to local trains, and these four-wheelers were designed for longer distance runs, with considerable stretches run without intermediate stops. The coach included a lavatory compartment, and also a warming apparatus. At the farther end can be seen the elevated brakesman's compartment. Externally the appearance of these carriages was as drab as the conditions inside. The dull grey paint was no more than faintly relieved by the vermilion lining, and like most Continental coaches of all periods they were rarely cleaned, and so lost every vestige of colour!

13 **Egyptian State Railways:** Second-class Carriage.

At the period covered by this book the Locomotive Superintendent of the Egyptian State Railways was F. H. Trevithick, a grandson of the great Cornish pioneer, and he had charge of carriage and wagon design and maintenance in addition to the locomotives. The type of second-class carriage illustrated was used on the ordinary, as distinct from the crack express trains, and is particularly interesting as being one of the earliest examples of a coach having steel underframing, and steel body framing. They were entered through doors on the end platforms. The roofs were double, the spacing between the inner and outer roof helping to keep the inside cool, while the windows were fitted with venetian blinds. Internally they were arranged compartment-wise with a central gangway from end to end. Very careful provision was made for ventilation. The main line northwards from Cairo to Alexandria is always subject to strong cross-winds, and running through continuous desert country would be most unpleasant if, in an attempt to get some relief from the heat, the train was run with the windows open. Taken all round, this is an excellent design of carriage, with an attractive exterior finish.

14 **Rhymney Railway:** Bogie Passenger Carriage.

In contrast to the local train carriages of most Continental countries British carriages of the period covered by this book were mostly very attractive in their external finish, even though they were often engaged on quite local services. In South Wales, for example, the Rhymney Railway, although primarily existing for the conveyance of coal from the mining valleys to Cardiff dock, operated a busy local passenger service, and the subject of our picture is a composite with three first- and four second-class compartments designed by Cornelius Lundie, the locomotive and carriage superintendent. Although possessing a fine works at Caerphilly for the repair and maintenance of the engines and rolling-stock, the new engines, carriages, and wagons were built by outside firms. The carriage illustrated was one built by the Gloucester Railway Carriage and Wagon Company. They were noteworthy for the time of their construction, 1901, by being lit by electricity, at a time when the majority of the British main line railways were still using gas for carriage lighting. For relatively short distance traffic the Rhymney Railway had no occasion to use corridor carriages.

15 **Paris, Lyons and Mediterranean Railway:** Four-cylinder Compound 4-4-0 Locomotive.

Following the successful introduction of the four-cylinder compound system of Alfred de Glehn on the Northern Railway of France other companies were quick to follow, and the Paris, Lyons, and Mediterranean Railway example illustrated was designed for working the increasingly popular express trains over the long main line from Paris to the French Riviera. The speeds demanded were not very high, and the provision of 'wind-cutter' fronts, wedge-shaped fronts to the cabs, and some aerodynamic fairing between the chimney and dome might have seemed little more than a publicity stunt. On the exposed stretches of line in Province, however, trains are subject to extremely high resistance from the Mistral wind, and anything that could be done to reduce air resistance was worth while. Between Arles and Marseilles thick hedges have been grown on both sides of the line to afford some shelter. The luxurious Riviera express, and the famous Cote d'Azur Pullman, made overall average speeds of about 50 m.p.h. between Paris and Nice. At that time engines were changed four times in the 536 miles between Paris and Marseilles: at Laroche, Dijon, Lyons, and Avignon. On each section one of these 'wind-cutter' compound 4-4-0s was used.

16 **Dutch State Railway:** 4-4-0 Express Passenger Locomotive.

For many years it had become traditional for the Dutch State Railway to purchase its locomotives from England. The State Railway was not the only system operating in Holland, and in fact there were four others, some of which used to favour German-built engines. In 1880 Beyer, Peacock & Co. supplied the first of the famous 2-4-0 express engines with outside frames, which in handsome appearance and performance on the road created an extremely good impression and paved the way for many more orders from the State Railway. So important a landmark was this design regarded in Dutch railway history that one of these engines has been preserved and is now on display at the Dutch Railway Museum at Utretcht. The 4-4-0 illustrated in our picture was a development, in the period of this book, from the historic 2-4-0s. They proved equally successful. Technically they had cylinders 18 in. diameter by 26 in. stroke; 7 ft. diameter coupled wheels and a total heating surface of $1302\frac{1}{2}$ sq. ft. The grate area was 22.6 sq. ft. But technicalities apart they were without much doubt among the most ornate and attractive-looking engines on the continent of Europe.

17 **Belgian State Railways:** The Scottish-built 4-4-0.

Towards the end of the nineteenth century the Belgian Government, though possessing many ingeniously designed locomotives, made a study of contemporary overseas practice, and decided to purchase five locomotives of the Caledonian 'Dunalastair' type, differing vastly from their own in the simplicity of the mechanical design and in the neatness of their external appearance. An approach was made to J. F. McIntosh, the Locomotive Superintendent of the Caledonian Railway, and while his board could not permit the locomotives to be built in their own works Mr McIntosh was instructed to provide all the necessary drawings and technical assistance so that the engines could be built at the neighbouring works of Neilson Reid & Co. one of the constituents of the North British Locomotive Co. Ltd. The five locomotives ordered by the Belgium Government differed from the Caledonian 'Dunalastair II' class only in having right-hand, instead of left-hand, drive, and certain small details. They were finished in the standard Caledonian style of the day and immediately established a great reputation on the Belgian railways. The design was very soon adopted as a national standard, and this development is illustrated on Plate 169.

18 **Chicago and North Western Railroad:** The 'Fast Mail' 4-4-0.

It was in 1899 that the Chicago and North Western Railroad put on the famous 'fast mail', making the night trip from Chicago to Omaha. It involved a good deal of very smart running, and some individual feats of performance, one imagines, became picturesquely exaggerated into 'World record' achievements. The 4-4-0 engines used were undoubtedly very free runners, and frequently exceeded 80 m.p.h. Dimensionally they were not so powerful as a Caledonian 'Dunalastair', as built for Belgium, but a number of interesting features are to be noted. The frames are of the 'bar' type, as distinct from the customary British plates; the cow-catcher is prominent, and the forward 'dome' carrying the number, 219, is not a steam dome at all, but a sandbox. A particular technical feature, which had not then been introduced in Great Britain was the taper boiler barrel—later to become standard on the English Great Western Railway. The cab was very large, and the driver sat high up on the right-hand side.

In making the through run of some 500 miles from Chicago to Omaha engines were changed twice, first at Clinton and then at Boone. Like most American locomotives of their period these Chicago and North Western Railroad 4-4-0s were painted plain black, though the boilers were left in their natural colour of 'blued steel'.

19 **Midland Railway:** 'Princess of Wales' Class 4-2-2.

The reintroduction of single-driver express locomotives on the Midland Railway was in large measure due to the invention of the steam sanding gear, which enabled slipping to be checked. The 'Princess of Wales' class, introduced in 1900, was the culmination of a gradual development from the first Johnson 4-2-2 single of 1887; there were ten in the class, and they differed from all the previous class 4-2-2s in having the large bogie tenders. At the turn of the century there was a general tendency in Great Britain to make increasingly long non-stop runs, and before the Midland Railway decided to instal water-troughs the use of large tenders was the only means available for providing the necessary water supply. The earlier tenders were adequate for non-stop running between St Pancras and Leicester (99 miles) or St Pancras and Nottingham (123 miles); but with the Yorkshire and Scottish expresses runs from London to Chesterfield, Rotherham, and even to Leeds (209 miles), were desired. The engines themselves were very powerful with cylinders 19½ in. diameter by 26 in. stroke; a total heating surface of 1217 sq. ft. and a grate area of 24.5 sq. ft. The driving wheels were 7 ft. 9½ in. diameter. The pioneer engine, No. 2601, *Princess of Wales*, was one of the only two Midland engines ever to bear names.

20 **Glasgow and South Western Railway:** A Stirling 0-4-2 as running *c.* 1903.

The family of Stirling was noted for the introduction of many splendid locomotives on a number of English and Scottish railways, and as constructed they were all characteristic by having domeless boilers. On the Glasgow and South Western Railway no less than ninety tough little 0-4-2s for mixed traffic duty were built by contractors between 1870 and 1878, and some thirty years later the frames and machinery of these was still in such excellent condition that James Stirling's successor, James Manson, rebuilt them with new and larger boilers of his own design giving them a neat and handsome appearance—quite up to date for a medium powered mixed traffic engine of the period. As such they became the 'maids-of-all-work' of the line, running fast goods, excursions, light express, and other miscellaneous duties. They were greatly appreciated by the drivers and firemen, because they steamed freely and could be thrashed unmercifully at times to combat bad weather conditions, or heavy loading. In external appearance they were typical of the quietly dignified style of finish that was standard on the Glasgow and South Western Railway in Manson's time—in some ways characteristic of the personality of the locomotive chief himself.

21 **Great Western Railway:** Rebuilt 2-4-0 Passenger Engine.

One of the most marked characteristics of British locomotive practice in the early years of the present century was the extent to which relatively old engines were modernized by simple processes of rebuilding, fitting boilers of new design that were becoming standardized on a number of different engine classes. On the Great Western Railway G. J. Churchward rebuilt a number of Dean passenger engines in this way, fitting his own domeless boilers and high raised Belpaire fireboxes to classes previously having the Dean boilers, with huge brass domes for steam collection. The engine illustrated was one of a class introduced originally in 1889 for working principally on the north main line between Wolverhampton and Birkenhead. This section includes some stiff gradients particularly in the 1 in 82 bank by which Wrexham is approached from the north. The engines had 18 in. by 24 in. cylinders, and 6 ft. diameter coupled wheels. As rebuilt with the Churchward domeless boiler they became extremely smart-looking, and smart working little engines, and on light passenger and secondary branch work of all kinds they put in many years of excellent running after their rebuilding in 1903.

22 **Great Northern Railway:** American-built 2-6-0 Mixed Traffic Engine.

Just at the end of the nineteenth century increased freight traffic on several of the British railways came at a time when the locomotive works, both railway and private builders, were fully occupied, and the Great Northern, together with the Midland and the Great Central, took the unprecedented step of ordering locomotives from the U.S.A. To obtain the quickest possible delivery, an order for twenty was placed with the Baldwin Locomotive Company of Philadelphia, and beyond specifying general capacity the detailed design was left to the manufacturers. Certain details, such as the buffers, couplings, vacuum brake, and notably the chimneys, were of standard Great Northern Railway pattern, and the sandboxes were placed below the running-plate. Otherwise it was a pure American design. They were intended for freight traffic in the West Riding, and were generally similar in capacity to the Ivatt standard 0-6-0 goods engines already at work on the line, but were of the 2-6-0 type. They had cylinders 18 in. diameter by 24 in. stroke; 5 ft. 1 in. coupled wheels and worked at a pressure of 175 lb. per sq. in. Being rather lightly built, they did not have the staying power of the standard English engines, and although they served their immediate purpose admirably their life was short.

23 **Manhattan Elevated Railway, New York:** 0-4-4 Tank Engine.

The problem of transport in the heart of great cities, which is experienced nowadays even with modern systems of roads, traffic signals, one-way streets and such-like was experienced no less in the nineteenth century, when congestion was caused by the great increase in slow horse-drawn traffic; and in days even before the introduction of electric trams attempts were made to relieve matters so far as personal movement was concerned by the construction of railways running on continuous elevated viaducts along some of the main thoroughfares. In Chicago the 'elevated' was mostly run along the back streets as close to the main streets as possible, but in New York the main streets were followed, and a most picturesque and noisy affair it was, with swarms of the little 0-4-4 tank engines illustrated in our picture puffing and rattling along the viaducts over the streets; constantly stopping and starting. So far as operation was concerned it was worked as a tramway, without signals, the driver keeping a sharp look-out towards the train in front, which was usually in sight. Station stops rarely exceeded fifteen seconds. The Manhattan 'elevated' was converted to electric traction in the early

1900s, and some of these 0-4-4 tank engines were sold to the Chinese Government.

24 **Furness Railway:** A 'Cleator' Class 0-6-2 Tank Engine.

Although the Furness Railway served some of the choicest parts of the English Lake District, and did a great deal to foster tourist traffic, it was primarily a freight carrier, and in addition to business connected with shipbuilding at Barrow and coal at Whitehaven, almost the whole district served by the line included many iron-ore mines, and prior to the First World War the output from these was, taken in the aggregate, very heavy. The district lying east of the main line on its most northerly stretches, and centred upon Egremont and Cleator Moor, was at one time very busy, and for this area W. F. Pettigrew introduced a class of 0-6-2 mineral tank engines in 1898. This was the first Furness engine class designed specifically for the iron-ore traffic, working over lines some of which were joint with the London and North Western Railway. For this reason they were known as the 'Cleator Tanks'. They were powerful engines for their day, having cylinders 18 in. diameter by 26 in. stroke; and coupled wheels only 4 ft. 8 in. which with a pressure of 150 lb. per sq. in. gave a usefully high starting tractive effort. They were essentially short haul engines, and their fuel and water capacity was small: $1\frac{1}{2}$ tons of coal and 1400 gallons of water. As our picture shows they were finished in the attractive 'iron-ore red' livery of the Furness Railway.

25 **Lynton and Barnstaple Railway:** Narrow-gauge 2-4-2 Tank Engine *Lyn*.

This picturesque little railway running on a rail gauge of 2 ft. was opened in 1898 to connect the seaside resorts of Lynton and Lynmouth on the very hilly North Devon coast, with the standard gauge line of the London and South Western Railway at Barnstaple. To open the line three 2-6-2 tank engines from Manning Wardle of Leeds were obtained; but after a year's running a fourth engine was required, and as circumstances precluded the obtaining of another English engine in the time demanded this little railway, like the Great Northern, Midland, and Great Central, went to the U.S.A., and the tank engine *Lyn* was delivered by Baldwins in record time. Although it gave a lot of trouble at first this American-built engine had a far longer life than its main line counterparts. It was still going strong when the Lynton and Barnstaple Railway became part of the Southern Railway in 1923, and our picture shows the engine in Southern colours. By main line standards it was a tiny little thing, weighing only 22 tons, having cylinders 10 in. diameter by 16 in. stroke, and coupled wheels only 2 ft. 9 in. diameter. It was still in service when the time came for the little railway to be closed in 1935. Then, after its long life, it was sold for scrap and fetched a mere £50.

26 **Rhondda and Swansea Bay Railway:** 2-4-2 Tank Engine.

One of the lesser-known independent railways of South Wales, this line made an end-on connection with the Taff Vale Railway at Treherbert at the head of the Rhondda Valley, and proceeded by the longest tunnel in Wales to a steeply graded line leading down to the coast. The entire length of the line, including several short branches, was no more than 20 miles, and it was opened to traffic in 1895. It had the advantage of opening with thoroughly modern equipment. Of the original locomotive stock of twenty-six only five were designed specifically for passenger service, and it is one of these that we illustrate. The remainder are mostly 0-6-2 tank engines of similar appearance, used in the heavy mineral traffic of the line. The passenger 2-4-2 tanks, and most of the coal 0-6-2 tanks, were built by Kitson & Co. of Leeds. Both classes had cylinders 18 in. diameter by 26 in. stroke, and while the passenger 2-4-2s had 5 ft. 3 in. diameter coupled wheels the coal 0-6-2s had 4 ft. 6 in. diameter. Some slightly larger 2-4-2s were introduced in 1897. Although the engine we illustrate belonged to little more than a local railway it is representative of many British tank engines of the period, and of the excellent products of the private locomotive builders, who in this case also did the detail designing of the engine.

27 **Perak Government Railway:** 4-4-0 Passenger Engine of 1893 Design.

Railways were first introduced in the Malay Peninsula in 1885 in the state of Perak, at which time the whole country was covered in dense jungle and such transport as existed was entirely by river. The various independent states, such as Selangor, Johore, Sungei Ujong, each had British advisers and in working towards the eventual federation of all the Malay states certain important features of standardization were adopted as small, and at first independent and unconnected railways were built in the separate states. One of the earliest standard classes of engine was a small 4-4-0 tank, originally built for Perak and afterwards adopted in Selangor, Singapore, and Malacca. From this design, known later as Class 'A', came a larger version 'B' in 1890, and this was subsequently adapted to a tender engine design, as illustrated in our picture. Nearly all these early Malayan engines were built by Hunslet. They were tiny little things by contemporary standards elsewhere, operating on the metre gauge, having cylinders only 12 in. diameter by 18 in. stroke; coupled wheels 3 ft. 3 in. diameter, and a total weight of engine in working order of only 22 tons. The huge headlight was a very necessary item of equipment in the jungle and it is on record that one of them was charged and derailed by a bull elephant, the tender being lifted completely clear of the track.

28 **Sungei Ujong Railway:** 4-4-2 Tank Engine of 1899.

This Malayan state for administration purposes was linked with Negri Sembilan in the 'nineties', but its once independent railway did not come into the Federated Malay States system until 1908. It was a tiny concern, and at that time became merely the Port Dickson branch of the Federated Malay States Railway. There were only four locomotives, but one of these has been chosen for illustration to show how, in so many parts of the world, the British locomotive building industry played its part. Engine No. 4 of the Sungei Ujong Railway was built in Glasgow by Dübs & Co. and a characteristic design of the period. In nominal tractive power it was slightly inferior to the Hunslet 4-4-0s on the Perak Railway and elsewhere in Malay, having the same sized cylinders, but coupled wheels of 3 ft. 6 in. diameter, and a boiler pressure of 130 lb. per sq. in., against 140. But it was a well-designed and efficient little engine, having an all-up weight of 28 tons. Although so relatively small, and remaining as isolated unit—the only engine in the Federated Malay States Railway 'K' class—it retained a useful sphere of activity and was not scrapped until 1926: a remarkable life of twenty-seven years for a unique engine.

29 **Burma Railways:** 4-4-4 Oil-burning Tank Engine of 1899.

Burma, although forming part of the British Indian Empire, was completely separate from the rest of the Indian railways by mountain ranges and an exceedingly dense and difficult country. The main line running northward from Rangoon to Mandalay was not unduly difficult, and the interesting locomotive illustrated was built for shorter distances from Rangoon. The design of the framing and suspension reflects the nature of the track in its severe curvature and light construction. The frames are outside, to permit of as much clear space between the wheels as possible, and although the total wheelbase of the engine was 26 ft. 2 in. the fixed wheelbase was only 6 ft. 7 in. The compensated type of suspension was used, as can be seen from the lever between the two pairs of coupled wheels. The cylinders were 14 in. diameter by 20 in. stroke, and the coupled wheels 4 ft. 5 in. diameter. Steam distribution was by the Joy valve gear, outside. The engine was arranged for oil-firing, using the Holden system, successfully developed in England on the Great Eastern Railway. This engine, which weighed 36½ tons in working order, was built by Neilson Reid & Co. in Glasgow.

30 **Federated Malay States Railway:** The 'G' Class 4-6-0 of 1899.

The rapid expansion of the railway system in Malaya and the increasing traffic, particularly in Perak led to the introduction of the 4-6-0 type, and after some experimental engines had been tried the very successful 'G' class was put into service in Perak and Selangor in 1899. Engines for the former state came from Hunslet, and those for Selangor from the neighbouring Leeds firm of Kitsons. Before the formation of the Federated Malay States Railways, Perak had purchased thirteen of the class, and Selangor, eight. All the latter were from Kitsons, but of the later ones Perak purchased the three imported in 1901 from Robert Stephenson and Co., and the six in 1902 from Neilson Reid. A further eleven were added to the combined stock in 1903–5 after formation of the Federated Malay States Railway, and two more, in 1904, on the Malacca Railway. Although not very large, they were excellent engines, and many of them remained in traffic until the late 1930s. They had cylinders 14½ in. diameter by 20 in. stroke, coupled wheels 4 ft. 3 in. diameter, and a total engine weight, in working order of 30 tons. In connection with the formation of the Federated Malay States Railway it is of interest to add that of the two main constituents the Perak Railway originally had its locomotive headquarters at Ipoh, in the mountainous country to the north, while the Selangor Railway was established at Kuala Lumpur, which became the headquarters of the entire system.

31 **London–Brighton and South Coast Railway:** Family Saloon.

In the later years of the nineteenth century in Great Britain families travelling together for lengthy holiday visits, with much luggage and attended by the family servants, used to engage many compartments of the ordinary coaches on long-distance trains, and it became customary for the major railway companies to construct special family saloons, with interiors designed to provide appropriate accommodation for family, servants, and luggage. An extremely hansome vehicle of this kind is that of the London–Brighton and South Coast Railway illustrated here. The Brighton did not, of course, provide for long-distance travel within its own system; but these saloons could be chartered for travel from 'anywhere to anywhere', and a patron of the Brighton Railway might take his family from East Grinstead to Lairg, on the farther north section of the Highland line, where there would be good deer-stalking or grouse-shooting. As the time approached for the opening of the grouse-shooting season many of these family saloons would congregate at Perth, presenting a variety of coach designs and colours from many different railways in Great Britain. The journeys in many cases must have been long and eventful as the saloons were shunted from one train to another at intermediate junctions. Very often the saloons formed part of little cavalcades of their own, including one or more horse-boxes. They remain a picturesque reminder of a colourful period of travel in Great Britain.

32 **Prussian State Railways:** Mail Van.

There is always a special interest in the conveyance of mail by railway, and the travelling post-office vans on British railways form a study of their own. This German example is no less interesting, though it has no apparatus for collecting and delivering mails while travelling at speed. Continental railway carriages, particularly those working in the nineteenth century, were not distinguished for their grace or elegance of external finish; but this six-wheeler has a striking character about it in its high clerestory roof; the cab for the mail guard at the end, and in its dignified green livery and lining. Like post-office vans in Great Britain it carries the insignia of Royal authority and patronage of the post, in the Prussian black eagle, symbol also of a famous Order of Knighthood. Otherwise the details are simple and spartanlike, and it will be noticed that the wheels are of wagon-type, spoked. No particular regard would seem to have been paid to quietness of travel for the mail sorters inside.

33 **Great Eastern Railway:** Milk Van.

The conveyance of milk on the railways of Great Britain has always been a traffic of high priority. The needs of London in this respect have always been exceptional, and the sheer volume of milk brought into London every day from quite distant parts of the country has needed special vehicles. These, over the years, have reflected the changing trends in the farming industry itself. At one time individual farmers contributed their quota at small country stations, and the vans so loaded would be attached to local trains for conveyance to main line junctions. For traffic of this area the smart four-wheeled van such as that illustrated would be ideal. It was just large enough for a one-station load. Such vans had to be suitable for fast running on express trains and they were fitted with automatic continuous brakes. In later years when milk began to be conveyed by road to concentration points it was of advantage to the railways to use larger vans, one variety of which was once described as 'like a prison on wheels'. Although it is stepping right outside our period one can refer to the modern practice of carrying milk in glass-lined tanks, filled full at the loading point, and discharged at the city milk distributing station.

34 **Austrian Four-wheeled Passenger Carriage.**

In the earliest days of railways much attention was paid to the wealthy passengers travelling first class, and although the details of carriage design were somewhat primitive and conducive to a jerky and bumpy ride the actual apartments were nicely furnished. It is true, little was done to provide good heating and ventilation. For the lower orders, however, railways all over the world provided the very least that they could. After the provision of covered carriages for the third-class passenger had been made compulsory in Great Britain in 1844, the carriages themselves were little more than wooden boxes. On the British railways a great reform began in 1876 when the Midland Railway abolished second class and converted all their cushioned 'seconds' into 'thirds'. But on the continent of Europe the change was much slower in coming, and the four-wheeled carriage illustrated was typical of many running in main line trains at the turn of the century. Like the Dutch and Prussian carriages illustrated on Plates 11 and 12 the exterior finish did little to relieve the generally drab effect. Such carriages were hardly ideal for seeing the magnificent mountain country, a hint of which is shown in the reflection in the windows.

35–38 **Nineteenth-century Austrian Locomotives.**

The Austrian railways were not brought under a single State administration until after the First World War, and at the period covered by this book a considerable change in general practice and appearance was in progress. The illustrations referring to these notes are both of the early and the transitional period. Although angular and having most of the fittings outside the earlier Austrian engines possessed great character and a fascination for the enthusiast.

35 **Austrian State Railway:** 4-4-0 Express Passenger Engine.

This illustrates a design introduced in 1885 and built at the Vienna Locomotive Works, a private company, because none of the Austrian railways built their own locomotives. The State Railway, or to give a literal translation of its full title, the Imperial Royal Austrian State Railway, ran westwards from Vienna to Salzburg, and thence by a circuitous route through the mountains to Worgl, in the Tyrol. Then the line of State ownership was interrupted by a section of the Southern Railway between Kufstein on the German frontier and the Brenner Pass. West of Innsbruck came the far-famed line through the heart of the Tyrol, passing through the Arlberg Tunnel. The small 4-4-0 class was used on the more level sections of the line between Vienna and Salzburg, though even there are to be found long stretches of gradual inclinations, as in the ascents at each end of the line—westwards through the hill country of the Vienna Woods, and eastwards from Salzburg through the foothills of the Salzkammergut Mountains

36 **Austrian State Railway:** Karl Gölsdorf's Two-cylinder Compound 4-4-0.

This extraordinary looking engine was the first of a remarkably successful series of compound engines. Gölsdorf, who between 1893 and 1916 designed no fewer than forty-six different types of locomotives, had already introduced his extremely simple system of compounding on a famous prototype—the 0-10-0 goods engine No. 180.01. He used only two cylinders, and they thus had to be different sizes, and the system had the merit from the maintenance point of view that everything was outisde, and easily 'get-at-able'. One of the most striking features of all the early Gölsdorf engines was the arrangement of double domes with a huge connecting pipe. One is familiar with the arrangement on American and other locomotives that *looks* like two, or more, domes, where in fact one only of the mountings is actually a dome, and the others are sandboxes. On the Gölsdorf engines they were both genuine domes. Steam was collected in the rear one, and then passed through the pipe to the forward one in which the regulator was mounted. From the illustration it will be seen that the crank operating the regulator valve was outside the forward dome, and worked by a long rod from the cab. Not a handsome engine, to English eyes, but one immensely full of character!

37 **Austrian Southern Railway:** 4-4-0 Express Locomotive.

The Südbahn was in two separate sections; one was that from Kufstein to the Brenner, previously mentioned, but the longer and perhaps more important was that running south from Vienna via the Semmering Pass to Italy and Servia. For this latter line the celebrated '17c' class of 4-4-0 was built in large numbers between 1855 and 1901. These were long-lived engines *in excelsis.* The photograph from which our illustration was prepared was taken by the author in the year 1964, when the engine was still in service on the privately-owned Graz–Köflacher Bahn, which is a largely mineral line connecting with the southern main line of the Austrian Federal Railways at Graz in Styria. Engaged in local light passenger work this veteran is working adjacent to the main line over which she and her class did such yeoman service more than sixty years ago. They were two-cylinder simples and were designed for a maximum speed of 55 m.p.h. The coal used would have been regarded as poor, by British standards, having a calorific value of not more than 10,000 B.Th.Us. per pound, compared with British values, with good bituminous coal of 13,000 to 14,000.

38 **Mountain 0-8-0 for the Arlberg Route.**

The line leading westward from Innsbruck to Switzerland via the Arlberg Tunnel is one of the most severe in Europe, and its major 'ramps' are inclined at 1 in 38 like those of the Gothard and Lötschberg routes in Switzerland. The engine illustrated is an 0-8-0 used for freight and rear-end banking on the principal gradients. A later illustration in this book (ref. 127) shows one of the 2-8-0s designed by Karl Gölsdorf for the express passenger trains; but these were not powerful enough to climb the 'ramps' unassisted. This freight engine is certainly no beauty. The sandbox on top of the boiler is a highly utilitarian affair, while the 'adornment' on the chimney is the Kobel spark arrester. One can well imagine that steam locomotives blasting their way up these steep gradients would, in the ordinary way, throw many sparks, and this could have caused serious fires in the dense forests through which much of the line passes on the mountain sections.

39 **Belfast and Northern Counties Railway: Ballymena and Larne Section,** 2-4-2 Compound Tank Engine.

The various narrow-gauge railways of Ireland, built in the 3 ft. gauge and many built under the provisions of a succession of Light Railway Acts of Parliament provide a fascinating variety of locomotives and rolling-stock. The Ballymena and Larne line was one of the most efficient, and even ran a 'boat express' in connection with the steamer sailings from Larne. The remarkable 2-4-2 tank engines illustrated were first introduced in 1892 during Mr Bowman Malcolm's long tenure of office as Locomotive Engineer of the Ballymena Northern Counties Railway. They were two-cylinder compounds on the Worsdell von Borries system and, of course, when seen from the front the different sized cylinders gave them a very odd look. They were excellent engines in traffic and after their own line was closed in the late 1920s they were transferred to the Ballycastle Railway, and did good work there until the Second World War. At that time they were in London, Midland, and Scottish ownership, forming part of the locomotive stock of the Northern Counties Committee. All Northern Countries engines were painted in Midland red. They were smartly kept and looked exceedingly fine. The cylinder diameters were 14¾ in. high pressure and 21 in. low pressure, with a common stroke of 20 in. The coupled wheel diameter was 3 ft. 9 in., and with a boiler pressure of 160 lb. per sq. in. they had the high tractive effort, for a small narrow gauge line, of 13,150 lb.

40 **Listowel and Ballybunion Railway:** 'Double' Engine.

This line was one of the great railway curiosities of the British Isles. The peculiar form of track construction was the invention of a Frenchman named Lartigue, and it was claimed to minimize the cost of track construction in countries where communication was needed, but where speed was of no consequence. The Listowel and Ballybunion Railway was built more as a demonstration of the system than anything else. It was only 9½ miles long, and connected a little coastal township in West Kerry with the town of Listowel on the Limerick and Tralee line. Everything had to be doubled, equally balanced on either side of the central trestle, and of course this requirement led to many tales of the devices resorted to in the case of awkward loads. A farmer wanted to send one cow; after much argument he was induced to send two calves as a balancing load on the outward journey, and then the two calves were returned, one on either side on the return trip! Of course the railway did not pay. It was opened in 1888, but was too remote and too little known to provide a tourist joke. To-day it could have been a railway enthusiast's mecca, but it was closed down in 1924, long before the present wave of interest began. In actual working the speed of running was 15 to 20 m.p.h. though the motion had an uneasy pitching character which made strangers to the line somewhat nervous.

41 **Donegal Railways:** 4-4-4 Tank Locomotive *Hercules.*

The Donegal Railways, which later became the County Donegal Railways Joint Committee, consisted of a sprawling group of lines making their way through various glens in the wild and sparsely populated mountain country of north-west Ireland from Londonderry and Strabane to Ballyshannon and Killybegs. Between Strabane and Londonderry the line roughly paralleled the broad gauge line of the Great Northern, the narrow gauge extension having been built to avoid the break of gauge at Strabane and the inconvenience of transhipping from the Donegal Railway proper goods that were bound for the port of Londonderry. As might be expected, a line that had grown up piecemeal had a varied assortment of locomotives, and the one chosen for illustration is one of a pair built by Neilson Reid & Co. in 1902. They were powerful engines for the narrow gauge, and the weight on their coupled wheels was too great for some of the bridges on the the mountain sections. But they did good work on the more level line north-eastwards from Stranorlar being rated to haul 325 tons. They had cylinders 14 in. diameter by 20 in. stroke; coupled wheels 4 ft. diameter, and a nominal tractive effort of 11,100 lb. They were both named. Engine No. 10 was named *Sir James*, after a director, and it will come as a surprise to readers to know that the subject of our picture *Hercules* was also a director, and not the character from Greek mythology. At that time Hercules was not an uncommon Christian name among the nobility and gentry of Ireland.

42 **Londonderry and Lough Swilly Railway:** 4-6-2 Tank Engine.

There was perhaps never a railway less aptly named than the 'Lough Swilly', unless it was the Anglo-Welsh–Manchester and Milford. The original project, dating from 1853, set out to do just what the name said, and it entailed a narrow gauge line 8½ miles long. By 1903 its extent had grown to 99½ miles, mainly in the form of a long westward extension of nearly 50 miles from Letterkenny to Burtonport. But still the old name persisted. In the early 1900s, in the absence of any competition, it was remarkably prosperous and paid a steady dividend of 7 per cent. Its locomotive stock was varied in most respects. It had some quite large tank engines of the 4-8-4 type, and some 4-8-0 tender engines, specially for working the long Burtonport extension line. Both these apply to a time rather outside our period, and the type chosen for illustration is one of a class of 4-6-2 tanks built by Hudswell, Clark & Co. and supplied in 1899. These handsome engines had cylinders 15 in. diameter by 22 in. stroke; coupled wheels 3 ft. 9 in. diameter, and having a nominal tractive effort of 14,050 lb. They were originally intended for the north line to Cardonagh, but proving generally useful were employed indiscriminantly over the whole system. Engine No. 7 of this class had the distinction of working a Royal Train, when King Edward VII and Queen Alexandra landed at Buncrana during a visit to Ireland in 1903 and travelled to Londonderry by train.

43 **Swedish State Railways:** Class 'Cc' 4-4-0 Locomotive of 1900.

This was the standard Swedish express passenger class for many years, and although it has such a distinctive and individual appearance, it is interesting to recall that the original design, of which these 4-4-0s of 1900 were a direct development, was entirely English, and dated back to 1856. In that year Beyer, Peacock & Co. supplied the first of the numerous 2-4-0s of the 'Västergötland' class, of which there were eventually 45, some built in England and others in Sweden. They were inside-framed with outside cylinders. From this design was developed the 4-4-0 type, which was first introduced in 1886. From this latter, which was another numerous class, came the engine illustrated. Apart from the 'collar' of the spark arrester, referred to in more detail under reference 134, these engines had a neat and graceful appearance, though the cabs were almost of American proportions, with protection at the rear as well, to shield enginemen from the rigours of the Scandinavian winters. These engines had cylinders 16½ in. diameter by 23¼ in. stroke, coupled wheels 6 ft. 2 in. diameter, and a boiler pressure of 156 lb. per sq. in. After about fifteen years' service their usefulness was increased by the addition of superheaters, and in all the class put in some forty years' service on the line. These engines were built in Sweden by Nydgvist and Holm.

44 **Swedish State Railways:** Class 'Kd' Standard 0-6-0 Goods Locomotive of 1900.

The State ownership of railways existed almost from the earliest days in Sweden, and one result of this was to produce a greater standardization of locomotive design than was to be seen elsewhere in the latter part of the nineteenth century. Once a design was reasonably successful—and there was no really fast running to extend passenger lococmotives to their limit—it was built in considerable numbers for general service throughout the country. The 0-6-0 goods engine of Class 'Kd' was the freight equivalent and exact contemporary of the 'Cc' 4-4-0 passenger engine. It had the same general characteristics, but with the addition of a sandbox on top of the boiler. Between the years 1890 and 1902 no fewer than 139 of these engines were built. The coupled wheel diameter was 4 ft. 6 in., and the cylinders were 16½ in. diameter by 23¾ in. stroke. The boiler pressure, as on the 4-4-0s, was 156 lb. per sq. in. In the earlier days of Swedish railways four-wheeled tenders were the rule, and these were also used with the 'Kd' 0-6-0s, as shown in our picture. A change to larger tenders came with the 4-4-0s of Class 'Cc'. Like the 4-4-0s, many of the standard 0-6-0s were rebuilt with new superheated boilers and had an equally long life. A medium powered 0-6-0 was always an extremely useful general service engine in the steam era; and these Swedish 0-6-0s were no exception.

45 **Swedish State Railways:** Class 'Mb' Iron Ore 2-8-0 Locomotive.

Useful though the 'Kd' class 0-6-0s were in general goods service, traffic on the Lapland Ore line was getting beyond the unaided capacity of them by the turn of the century and some powerful new 2-8-0s were designed specially for the job. Until this time, although a considerable number of locomotives had been *built* in Sweden the design influences had been mainly British and German, and as mentioned in reference 46, American. But the Lapland Ore 2-8-0s were of wholly Swedish design, and it is interesting to find that for this hard-slogging, slow work, the engines were built as two-cylinder compounds, using the Walschaerts valve gear, outside. The cylinder diameters were 21 in. high pressure and 32 in. low pressure, with a common stroke of 25 in., and the coupled wheel diameter was 4 ft. 3 in. The first series of these engines, Class 'Ma', was turned out in 1901, and had a boiler pressure of 200 lb. per sq. in.; the second series, which is illustrated in our picture, had slightly smaller boilers carrying a pressure of 175 lb. per sq. in. They were large engines for their day having a total weight in working order of 76¾ tons, without their tenders. Apart from these engines the 0-6-0 remained the standard for goods on the State Railways for another six years, then construction of 0-8-0s began.

46 **Swedish State Railways:** Class 'Ta' Compound 4-6-0 Locomotive.

The years 1899–1901 witnessed a locomotive 'famine' in many parts of Europe, and whereas the large manufacturing firms in Great Britain, France, Germany, and elsewhere had been able to meet not only the needs of their own railways, but to support a large export trade, at this period their manufacturing capacity was saturated. Even in Great Britain recourse had to be made to supplies from outside Europe. It was at this time that the first American engines were imported into Sweden. Unlike the contemporary British imports, which were of medium powered goods engines, the new arrivals from the Richmond Locomotive Works of Richmond, Virginia, were the largest and most powerful engines yet to run the rails in Sweden. They were 4-6-0s having a general appearance not unlike the Lapland Ore 2-8-0s, with the addition of a sandbox on the boiler top. Like these latter, also, they were two-cylinder compounds, and being in general service, more within the sight and hearing of the general public than the 2-8-0s in the remote north, they attracted much attention from what has been described as 'their slow, breathless-sounding exhausts': only two beats per revolution instead of the usual four. The cylinder diameters were $22\frac{3}{4}$ in. high pressure, and 31 in. low pressure, with a common stroke of 24 in.; the coupled wheel diameter was 5 ft. 2 in., and the boiler pressure 200 lb. per sq. in.

47 **New York Central Railroad:** 2-6-6 Tank Engine.

This line, of which the full original title was the New York Central and Hudson River Railroad, forms the first link in one of the most famous and heavily worked routes from New York to Chicago. Although the ultimate direction is from east to west, the first lengthy stretch is almost due north following a level course beside the Hudson River. In addition to its long-distance express trains the New York Central operated a heavy suburban traffic, and the interesting locomotive illustrated was one of a series introduced at the end of 1902. Typically American in appearance, with a sandbox on the boiler top, large headlight and bell, and a commodious all-embracing cab, it is nevertheless unusual in having the coal bunker and tank supported on a six-wheeled trailing bogie. The coal and water capacity of this tank engine was indeed equal to that of many British long-distance express engines of the day: 4 tons of coal and 3500 gallons of water. The cylinders (two in number) were 20 in. diameter by 24 in. stroke; the coupled wheels 5 ft. 3 in. diameter, and the boiler and firebox had a heating surface of 2432 sq. ft. The total weight in working order of this massive engine was 101 tons.

48 **Great Northern Railway:** 0-8-2 Tank Engine for London Metropolitan Traffic.

In the early 1900s railways were becoming increasingly aware of the danger of competition from road services in large towns, local electric railways, trams, and such-like, and the Great Northern, following the notable Great Eastern experiment with the 'Decapod' (ref. 49) produced a powerful 0-8-2 tank engine. This was primarily intended for the considerable flow of freight traffic between the north and south of the river Thames, via the Metropolitan line and the South Eastern and Chatham Railway, via Ludgate Hill and Herne Hill. This is a section of heavy gradients, and one on which the locomotives were required to condense their exhaust in the tunnels of the Metropolitan line between King's Cross and Ludgate Hill. The engine illustrated was virtually a tank engine equivalent of the

Ivatt main line 0-8-0 mineral engines, with cylinders 20 in. diameter by 26 in. stroke and 4 ft. $7\frac{1}{2}$ in. coupled wheels. Engines of this class were also used on some suburban passenger trains, requiring rapid acceleration from rest. These large 0-8-2 tanks did not prove successful in the London area, where it was found 0-6-2 and 0-6-0 engines were more suitable; but they performed very many years of hard service in the Nottinghamshire coalfield area.

49 **Great Eastern Railway:** The Decapod.

In the early 1900s the advocates of electric traction were loud in stressing the advantages to be gained in heavy suburban traffic, particularly in rapidity of acceleration from rest. The Great Eastern conveyed from Liverpool Street the heaviest suburban traffic in the world, but its engineers were not convinced that electric traction was the ultimate answer, especially in respect of the high capital cost. And so the Locomotive Superintendent, James Holden, produced a special locomotive to accelerate a 300-ton train from rest to 30 m.p.h. in 30 seconds. It was an enormous engine for its day having ten coupled wheels; three cylinders of $18\frac{1}{2}$ in. diameter by 24 in. stroke, and a boiler with the then-unheard of heating surface, on a British locomotive of 3010 sq. ft. The firebox was proportionally large, with a grate area of 42 sq. ft. This remarkable engine was completed at Stratford Works in December 1902, and on trials fully justified the powers of acceleration predicted. It was, of course, vastly in advance of its time, but showed clearly enough that anything then claimed for electric traction could be achieved with steam. No more was heard of electrifying the Liverpool Street lines until more than thirty years later. There was no regular work for the 'Decapod' having made its demonstration runs, and it was scrapped after a short life.

50 **North Western Railway of India:** 2-8-2 Tank Engine.

This powerful engine represents one of the very few classes built for India, in the period of this book, outside the United Kingdom. Designed for service on the Mushkaf Bolan frontier section, which is heavily graded, it was built by the then Pittsburgh Locomotive Works, U.S.A., though many detail parts, including the steel for tyres, axles, and cranks pins, were supplied from England. The complete locomotives were a combination of British and American practice; the generally neat outline and inside valve gear being British, while the sandboxes on top of the boiler spaced equally either side of the dome, were American. The single slide bar, with suspended crosshead, will also be noted. The frames were of the bar type, as largely standard in America. They were powerful engines, with cylinders 20 in. diameter by 26 in. stroke; a large boiler, with a total heating surface of 2090 sq. ft. and a grate very large by prevailing standards—30 sq. ft.—designed to burn Indian bituminous coal. The total weight of the engine in working order was $95\frac{3}{4}$ tons. While lying outside the general style of Indian locomotives at the turn of the century, this class forms an interesting counterpart to the American locomotives of the 2.6.0 type purchased for service in England at about the same time.

51 **Northern Railway of France:** Four-cylinder Compound Express 4-4-0.

The de Glehn compound system, briefly referred to in our reference to the Paris,

Lyons and Mediterranean 'wind-cutter' 4-4-0 (ref. 15), was virtually born on the Nord, where M. du Bousquet was anxious to improve the old 'Outrance' 4-4-0s (ref. 5). The first de Glehn compound was produced as a four-cylinder version of the Outrance, with the important feature that the drive was divided between the two coupled axles, thereby lessening the loads to be transmitted through the individual axles and bearings, and so lessening the chances of heating and breakage. On the Nord, the fruitful co-operation between M. du Bousquet and the English engineer Alfred de Glehn produced a series of splendid compound engines of which the example illustrated is one of the largest variety of 4-4-0 introduced in 1898. In France, until the introduction of colour light signalling in the 1930s, there was an overall speed limit of 120 km.p.h. (74½ m.p.h.) enforced by law, and to maintain the fast schedules with the English boat trains meant going hard uphill. This the Nord compound 4-4-0s did most efficiently sustaining speeds of 55 m.p.h. up the long 1 in 200 grades south of Amiens with train loads of 150 to 200 tons. They were fine, free-running engines, and could readily have exceeded the 74½ m.p.h. limit if permitted to do so.

52 **Prussian State Railway:** Two-cylinder Compound Express 4-4-0.

These interesting engines, with cylinders of two different sizes were entrusted with some of the fastest running schedules in Germany at the turn of the century. Generally speaking German speeds were relatively low particularly in the southern states; but the Prussian State had an express booked to cover the 99 miles from Hamburg to Wittenberge in 113 minutes and to cover the remaining 78¾ miles to Berlin in 91 minutes. The respective averages, in each case, start to stop, were 52½ and 52 m.p.h. The loads were usually around 170 to 200 tons, which were heavy for so relatively slender a locomotive. The cylinders were 18½ in. diameter high pressure and 26¾ in. low pressure, with a common stroke of 23½ in., coupled wheels were 6 ft. 6 in. diameter, and total heating surface 1250 sq. ft. The boiler pressure was relatively low for a Continental compound of that period, 175 lb. per sq. in. External features were the square sandbox on the boiler top just behind the dome and the Walschaerts valve gear. These engines did their work well, though they were soon to be superseded by the powerful superheater compound 4-4-0s described under reference 142.

53 **Jura–Simplon Railway:** Two-cylinder Compound 4-4-0.

It would be a fascinating experience if one could place along side each other, or perhaps better still group round the central turn-table of an old-time roundhouse, representative examples of the locomotives of all the countries of Europe running at one particular date in history. By far the greatest variety would have been seen from the old individual railway companies of Great Britain and Ireland; but in our plates 51–54 are shown four highly distinctive examples of Continental express passenger engines. Significantly, all are compounds, yet it was only the de Glehn type as developed to such advantage in France that really survived the test of time. None of the European railways, except the French, were yet running hard in the early 1900s; but in England and Scotland, where there was already much fast and hard work to be done the compound was not generally favoured. The Swiss engines illustrated in our picture worked on the comparatively level main line that runs beside the Lake of Geneva and up the Rhône Valley to Brigue. Although cutting through exceedingly mountainous country the changes in level of the course of the Rhone are no more than gradual. When this route became a through artery for international traffic after the opening of the Simplon Tunnel these 4-4-0s were superseded on the heaviest trains by the 4-6-0s (ref. 176).

54 **Vladikawska Railway, Russia:** Two-cylinder Compound 4-6-0 Express Locomotive.

This essentially functional, though nevertheless handsome, design of locomotive was introduced for working international express trains on the Russian stages of their journeys, and were built in Hanover. Like so many engines of the day on the continent of Europe they were compounds, with only two cylinders. The high raised running-plate, with all the running gear exposed is characteristic of a style that was virtually unknown in Great Britain at the time, but which, in the last years of steam, became the acknowledged standard. These Russian engines had slide valves, and the variety illustrated in our picture had the English-designed Joy valve gear, with its connection to the mid-point of the connecting-rod. This ingenious arrangement, which was standard on the London and North Western Railway for many years, avoided the need for eccentrics and greatly simplified the gear. On the Russian engine it is all arranged outside. Other engines of this class had the Walschaerts gear. The rails along the high running-plate and round the engine front were a Russian characteristic of the day. The cylinder diameters were 19¾ in. high pressure and 29 in. low pressure, with a common stroke of 26 in.; the coupled wheel diameter was 6 ft. 1 in. and the total heating surface 1630 sq. ft.—altogether a very workmanlike and attractive locomotive.

55 **Great Southern and Western Railway, Ireland:** 4-4-0 Express Passenger Engine.

Apart from its general services in the south-west of Ireland, the Great Southern and Western Railway had a twofold importance as a trunk route: first in the conveyance of the American mails put ashore at Queenstown and carried to Kingstown for connection with the Irish Mail service to London; and secondly as a tourist route between Dublin and Killarney. These handsome 4-4-0s, designed by Robert Coey and put on the road in 1903, were intended for both these trunk line services, and included non-stop running over the entire length of the Killarney branch from Mallow. The locomotive department of the Great Southern and Western Railway based much of its practice on that of Crewe, and the similarity in style of these 4-4-0s to engines of the London and North Western Railway will be apparent. As a powerful non-compound 4-4-0, however, they actually preceded the famous 'Precursors' of George Whale by about a year. The Irish engine had 18 in. by 26 in. cylinders, but a moderate boiler with only 1275 sq. ft. of heating surface, and 21 sq. ft. of grate area. All the coal used on the Great Southern and Western Railway was imported from Wales. It is of added interest to recall that at the time these engines were designed and built at Inchicore Works Mr R. E. L. Maunsell, later famous as the Chief Mechanical Engineer of the Southern Railway of England, was Works Manager.

56 **Great Southern and Western Railway, Ireland:** A Bogie Brake-Composite Carriage.

The Great Southern and Western Railway, like the other Irish main line railways of sixty or seventy years ago, worked in close collaboration with the English companies working the cross-Channel packet services, and the Great Southern and Western Railway had a double, and somewhat conflicting, allegiance to the London and North Western Railway in its partnership in the American mail service via Queenstown, Kingstown, and the Irish Mail route to Euston, and to the Great Western in respect of the Fishguard–Rosslare service. The Great Southern and Western Railway was also developing a series of through-carriage services, like the Great Western, that required a completely self-contained vehicle—first- and third-class compartments, and a brake and luggage van. A good example is shown in our picture. Until the end of the nineteenth century Great Southern and Western Railway carriages were finished in a dark 'plum' colour; but to match in some ways the smart two-tone finishes of their English associates a very distinctive style was adopted early in the present century, using white upper panels, a smart purple-brown for the bodies—much lighter and brighter than those of the London and North Western Railway—while the window surrounds and panelling included bright blue lining.

57 **Midland Great Western Railway, Ireland:** 4-4-0 Express Locomotive.

The locomotive practice of the principal Irish railways tended to follow that current in Great Britain, but in this respect, and particularly in regard to finish, the Midland Great Western Railway stood alone. While the Great Southern and Western had a style similar to that of the English London and North Western Railway, and the Great Northern followed the English Great Northern, the Midland Great Western Railway in its very handsome blue had its nearest English counterpart in the Somerset and Dorset joint. The Irish engines were rather more ornate, with brass bands over the coupled wheel splashers, and a scarlet background to the number-plates. The engine illustrated is one of a class introduced in 1902, designed by E. Cusack, and built at the company's works at Broadstone, Dublin. Speeds scheduled were not high, but these engines could run fast when required. They had cylinders 18 in. diameter by 26 in. stroke; coupled wheels 6 ft. 3 in. diameter; total heating surface 1363 sq. ft.; and a working pressure of 180 lb. per sq. in. Their designed performance was a speed of 60 m.p.h. on level track with a load of 310 tons behind the tender, and 30 m.p.h. up a gradient of 1 in 100, with a trailing load of 280 tons. These engines had the added interest of attractive names.

58 **Midland Great Western Railway, Ireland:** Corridor Carriage.

Shortly after the turn of the century the Midland Great Western Railway put into service some extremely fine new stock for the mail trains running between Dublin and Galway. This line, running across Ireland from east to west, was like the other trunk lines in the country in that its principal express trains were timed to provide connection with the Irish Mail service between London and Dublin, so that there was sufficient time at the furthest main line destinations in Ireland, such as Cork and Galway, for a business man to receive a letter posted in London on the previous day and to send a reply by the up 'Limited Mail' service in the late afternoon which would catch the night mail from Dublin to London. The Midland Great Western Limited Mail, when composed of new corridor stock introduced in 1902, consisted of a minimum of seven coaches including dining-car. It is interesting to recall that while all other vehicles in the train had elliptical roofs the dining-cars were of the clerestory type. It is also significant of the amount of luggage then carried by passengers that although these mail trains had only four coaches providing seating other than the dining-cars, a 58 ft. 'full brake' van was included. The two train sets allocated to the mail service had different internal upholstery, one being finished in royal blue and the other in old gold.

59 **East Indian Railway:** Standard 4-4-0 Express Locomotive.

This railway, one of the largest and most important in India, ran westwards from its headquarters in Calcutta to serve the principal cities in what could be termed Central Northern India, and in 1900 it had a route mileage of nearly 3000. The express locomotive illustrated, the characteristics of which are wholly British, was designed by A. W. Rendell, and was one of a class of fifty introduced in 1893-4. At that time traffic was booming and the contract was divided between the two Glasgow firms of Neilson Reid and Dübs—twenty-five to each. This procedure anticipated by thirty-four years what was done with the famous order for 'Royal Scot' 4-6-0s by the London Midland, and Scottish Railway. This was placed with the North British Locomotive Company, and because of its urgency twenty-five were built in each of the Hyde Park and Glasgow Park works, which were, of course, the establishments of Neilsons and Dübs respectively before those firms amalgamated with Sharp Stewart & Co. to form the North British Locomotive Co. Ltd. The East Indian 4-4-0s of 1893 had cylinders 18 in. diameter by 26 in. stoke; 6 ft. 7 in. coupled wheels; a total heating surface of 1241 sq. ft., and a grate area of 24 sq. ft. The rail gauge was the standard Indian for principal main lines of 5 ft. 6 in.

60 **Great Indian Peninsula Railway:** Old-style Passenger Brake Van.

One could not seek a greater contrast in passenger rolling-stock anywhere in the world than the old and new passenger train brake vans of the Great Indian Peninsula Railway, as shown in this illustration and that under reference 61. The old one is an example of the earliest days of third-class passenger travel in India, while the magnificent bogie carriage was in many ways a pioneer, rather than typical of the early twentieth century. The old four-wheeler shows very clearly the traditional form of 'sun-shade' that was fitted to almost all passenger vehicles in India. The guard's door had the awning cut away, presumably to allow him to look up and down the train; but the passengers had to duck under the awning to reach the door for their compartments. The picture shows how the body was mounted on two large baulks of timber forming the frame. There was no continuous brake, and the brake blocks, which were applied by hand, were of hard wood. It was altogether a very primitive affair, but a number of them were still in service at the end of the nineteenth century, on secondary services, of course.

61 **Great Indian Peninsula Railway:** Bogie-brake Third Carriage.

The introduction of this splendid range of bogie carriage stock in 1904–5 marked the beginning of a new trend in Indian carriage design. Although the carriage illustrated under reference 60 is a very primitive type it includes the awning or sun-shade which was a standard feature of all Indian passenger stock until the early 1900s, whether these were non-bogie, non-corridor vehicles for native passengers, or the most luxurious coaches for the mail trains. The engineer responsible for the notable change on the Great Indian Peninsula Railway was Mr A. M. Bell, the resident Carriage and Wagon Superintendent. He also broke away from another long established Indian tradition whereby carriages were painted different colours to denote the class—doubtless to assist illiterate native passengers. A popular colour scheme was white for first class, dark green for second class, and dark red for third class, all with red brown sun-shades. Mr Bell used the beautiful colour schemes illustrated for all passenger carriages. Instead of the sun-shades a layer of non-conducting material was inserted between the inner and outer lining of the roof and sides. These coaches were put into service on the Bombay-Poona mail trains, which had the fastest running schedules in India, with several intermediate runs made at about 50 m.p.h. start to stop.

62 **Great Indian Peninsula Railway:** 4-4-0 Express Passenger and Mail Engine.

These very handsome and numerous engines formed the standard class for the most important express passenger and mail services on the Great Indian Peninsula Railway. The line running eastwards from Bombay formed the first link in the line of cross-continental communication from the ocean terminal from England to Delhi, Calcutta, and the east coast. For many travellers the Great Indian Peninsula Railway was the first contact with Indian railways, and the locomotives were always maintained in a high state of mechanical efficiency and immaculate turn-out. Apart from the unusual form of cab window and the cow-catcher the appearance was that of a perfect British design of the period, with straight running-plate, deep coupled wheel splashers, inside cylinders, and characteristically neat boiler mountings. Technically they had 18 in. by 26 in. cylinders; coupled wheels 6 ft. 7 in. diameter, and worked at a pressure of 160 lb. per sq. in. The livery followed closely that of the London–Brighton and South Coast Railway in Earle Marsh's time. There were fifty of these engines in service, though at the end of our period they were beginning to be superseded by Mr Sarjant's large new 'Atlantics' (ref. 115).

63 **Shanghai–Nanking Railway:** Coat of Arms.

This line, a product of British railway enterprise, was constructed in the early years of the present century, and had a main line of 193 miles connecting the two cities included in its name. It was one of the so-called Concession railways, built with British capital secured by Imperial Chinese Bonds with the railway itself as first mortgage security. Construction began in 1905, and the line was finally completed in 1908 when the long tunnel at Chinkiang was finished. The railway was equipped in splendid style, with spacious layouts for even the smallest of wayside stations. The management was entirely British, and some of its fine locomotives and rolling-stock are illustrated elsewhere in this book. The line was built in the days of the old Imperial Government of China. After the revolution of 1911 which resulted in China becoming a republic, the Shanghai–Nanking line became part of the Chinese Government Railways though for many years subsequently remaining under British management. The quaint and original 'coat of arms' with the flags of Imperial China and of the United Kingdom, placed in juxtaposition with a pagoda, eloquently symbolizes the origin and early history of this finely equipped railway.

64 **Madras Railway:** Coat of Arms.

By the turn of the century there was quite a tangle of railway lines in Southern India, some on the broad gauge standard of 5 ft. 6 in., others on the metre gauge. Of these the Madras was unquestionably the most important based on the Bay of Bengal. From its terminal point in Madras itself there were two main routes, one running north-westward to make an end-on junction with the Great Indian Peninsula Railway at Raichur, and the other running south-westward right across the peninsula to reach the Indian Ocean at Calicut. The line to Raichur was most important as it formed part of the main route between Bombay and Madras 794 miles. Raichur was almost half-way between the two cities. The distance to Calicut from Madras was 413 miles. Speeds were not high, and the crack express train between Bombay and Madras then took 14¾ hr. to cover the 351 miles from Raichur to Madras. The coat of arms of the Madras Railway includes a 0-6-0 locomotive with a wood-burning smokestack, while the arms of the United Kingdom and of Madras itself rest against the stem of a coconut palm. In more recent years there was an amalgamation between the Madras and one of its narrow-gauge neighbours to form the Madras and Southern Mahratta Railway.

65 **Great Northern Railway, Ireland:** Coat of Arms.

The Irish railways in the nineteenth century kept very much in line with English and Scottish practices, and there was a certain amount of interchange of staff. Some of the most distinguished locomotive engineers of the day spent part of their careers in Ireland. In the designing of their coats of arms traditional practice was followed, and the Great Northern insignia indicates very clearly the principal centres served by the line. The main line, which after the establishment of the independent state of Eire became international, ran between Belfast and Dublin, and these are both prominently represented. The three twin-turreted castles, which also appear in a slightly different rendering on the coat of arms of the Great Southern and Western, is the coat of arms of the city of Dublin, while the ship on the rough sea heraldically described as 'a ship with sails set argent on waves of the sea proper' is part of the arms of Belfast. The city of Londonderry appears in the top right-hand quarter, while in the bottom left-hand quarter is the old crest of the borough of Enniskillen. This castle with portcullis flying the cross of St George is taken from the badge of the several Inniskilling regiments. Prominent among the city and town crests is the well-known Red Hand of Ulster.

66 **Great Southern and Western Railway:** Coat of Arms.

This was the largest of the Irish railways prior to the grouping of the British railways. The coat of arms dates from the nineteenth century before the company had absorbed the Waterford, Limerick, and Western. One feels that Waterford would certainly have been included, otherwise. The main line ran from Dublin to Cork, the crests of which are to be seen in the top left and bottom right quarters of the G.S. & W.R. coat of arms. The other crests incorporated are those of Kilkenny (top right) and Limerick (bottom left) The G.S. & W.R. had strong traffic associations with the English Great Western Railway, and the four separate shields are embraced in a quarter very similar in shape to that used in the G.W.R. up to the early 1930s. How the surrounding garter came to be abandoned is an interesting story, connected with the obtaining of Royal permission for the name *King George V* to be used on the famous English 4-6-0 No. 6000. Very high authority came to observe the coat of arms on the tender, encircled in a garter. It was not so much the contents but the garter itself to which the exception was taken heraldically, and from that time onwards its use was discontinued on the G.W.R.

67 **New South Wales Government Railways:** The 'M40' Class 4-4-2 Suburban Tank Engine.

These engines were perhaps the most British-looking of all New South Wales locomotives of the period. They were designed for the Sydney suburban services, and particularly for the steeply graded Hornsby and South Shore lines. There were fifteen in the class, built by Beyer, Peacock & Co. They had 17 in. diameter cylinders, with 26 in. stroke, and 5 ft. diameter wheels. They were excellent engines in their day, but rather quickly became overpowered by the rapid increase in the loads of the Sydney suburban trains. The great success of the 'P6' class 4-6-0 main line engines led to the designing of a 4-6-4 suburban tank engine in the same tradition and with the same 'family look', and these powerful new engines took over from the 4-4-2 tanks of Class 'M40' in the early 1900s. The 4-6-4s had 18½ in. by 24 in. cylinders, 4 ft. 7 in. coupled wheels, and a nominal tractive effort of 19,100 lb. which gave them a handsome advantage over the 'M40' class which had only 15,000 lb. of tractive effort. Regarding the 4-4-2 tanks, four were sold to private railways between 1918 and 1926 and the remainder were scrapped in 1925-7. Nevertheless, although they were outclassed on the duties for which they were originally introduced, a life of thirty years is a tribute to their general usefulness.

68 **New South Wales Government Railways:** The Celebrated 'P6' Class 4-6-0 Passenger Engine.

The New South Wales Government Railways, consisting of a fan-work of lines radiating in almost every direction from the great city of Sydney, has always been one of the busiest in Australia. In 1891 much larger engines than the existing 4-4-0s were needed, and the detailed design and supply of fifty engines of a new class were entrusted to Beyer, Peacock & Co. of Manchester. Apart from details of the cab and boiler mountings these engines bore a remarkable likeness to the Jones goods 4-6-0s of the Highland Railway, which were built by Sharp Stewart & Co. three years later. A particular point of similarity was the use of the Allan straight-link valve gear. The 'P6' class had cylinders 20 in. diameter by 26 in. stroke, and 5 ft. diameter coupled wheels, and eventually there were no fewer than 191 in service. The first fifty, built in England, had six-wheeled tenders, as shown in our picture, but later examples, some of which were built in the U.S.A., had eight-wheeled bogie tenders. As recently as 1954 all the 191 engines of this class were still in service, though since then, under the onset of dieselization, the majority have been scrapped. In the course of their long careers of more than sixty years they have been modernized by the fitting of superheaters and piston valves in place of the original slide valves. Even with these modifications they still remained vintage engines, and in any case one of the most remarkable steam-engine classes ever to run in Australia.

69 **New South Wales Government Railways:** The 'T524' Class 2-8-0 Goods Engine.

This very numerous class was the freight equivalent of the 'P6' 4-6-0 passenger type, and was a very powerful engine for the year of its introduction, 1896. Like the 'P6', the detail designing was done by Beyer, Peacock & Co., and the class bore a strong family likeness to it. They had 21 in. diameter cylinders, with a stroke of 26 in. and with coupled wheels 4 ft. 3 in. diameter, and a boiler pressure of 160 lb. per sq. in., the nominal tractive effort was 28,800 lb.—considerably greater than that of any British goods engine that had been built by that time. A first batch of five was supplied from England in 1896. These proved an immediate success, and further batches were ordered up to the year 1916. All except the last lot of thirty-one were imported from the United Kingdom as follows:

Beyer, Peacock & Co., Manchester	150
Neilson Reid & Co., Glasgow	10
Dübs & Co., Glasgow	5
North British Locomotive Co. Ltd.	84

The last thirty-one were ordered from the Clyde Engineering Co., which contrary to expectations was established not in Glasgow but in Sydney. By 1916 the total strength of the class was 280. Of these no less than 220 were still in service in 1954.

70 **New South Wales Government Railways:** Second-class Non-corridor Lavatory Carriage.

After the pioneer days had passed Australia railway carriage design appeared to be under a kind of dual influence. For long main line journeys and the interstate services the American Pullman type of car was favoured, whereas for shorter distances and suburban workings, the pattern was definitely British. The coach shown in our picture could have belonged to many of the British main line companies at the turn of the century, being entirely of the compartment type, and of characteristic construction with panelled sides and a generous amount of gold lining. Although running on the 4 ft. 8½ in. gauge standard in New South Wales, the overall width is narrower than many a British coach, and the non-corridor compartments seated five aside. Every compartment had access to a lavatory, which was not always the case on many British non-corridor carriages of the same period. Construction was very light, and although measuring 52 ft. 6 in. over buffers, the tare weight was only 22½ tons.

71 **Great Southern Railway of Spain:** Scottish-built 2-6-0 Engine of 1889–1905 Period.

This railway with the high-sounding name was actually a very small affair in the south, serving only the three towns of Baza, Lorca, and Aguilas, and it formed only one link in the chain of railway communication between Granada and Alicante. British influence was strong, and in 1889 delivery commenced of a series of 2-6-0 locomotives, one of which is the subject of our picture. Neilson's had the first order, for twelve, delivered in 1889–90; then followed two more, from Kitsons of Leeds in 1894; five from Sharp Stewart in 1901, and finally six from the North British Locomotive Co. Ltd. in 1905—twenty-five in all. It is believed that all of them are still in service on the line for which they were designed nearly eighty years ago! As will be seen from the picture, they are throughly British in appearance, and during their long life no change has been made to the boiler mountings and general equipment. Today they look just as typically 'nineteenth-century British' as the day they were first delivered. They are not large engines, having cylinders 18 in. diameter by 24 in. stroke; coupled wheels 4 ft. 9 in. diameter, and a total weight of engine and tender in working order of 81½ tons. To their orignal owners they must have proved a remarkably 'good buy'.

72 **Northern Railway of Spain:** 4-6-0 Passenger Engine of 1901–3.

The Northern Railway, the Norte, was one of the largest and most extensive constituents of the present Spanish National system, and as its name would suggest ran northwards from Madrid to the ports on the Bay of Biscay, and from Miranda extended eastwards to Zaragoza, Barcelona, and then southwards to Valencia. The engine illustrated is of the first 4-6-0 class introduced by the Norte, and built in Germany. Although very 'continental' in appearance, and so contrasting with the British-built 2-6-0s of the Great Southern, these engines are distinctly neater than many German locomotives of the period. They proved extremely successful in service. Originally ten were built by Hanomag of Hanover–Linden in 1901. Another eight were added from the same firm in 1902, followed by ten from Borsig of Berlin in 1903. This was not all. Modified only in the smallest detail, another ninety were added to the stock between the years 1904 and 1913, and the majority are still at work today. Unlike many Continental engines they were two-cylinder simples, with cylinder dimensions of which the English equivalents were roughly 19 in. diameter by 26 in. stroke, and the coupled wheel diameter is 5 ft. 1½ in.

73 **Madrid, Zaragoza, and Alicante Railway:** Four-cylinder Compound 4-6-0.

This was a railway that rather belied its name, and unlike the diminutive Great Southern, it had an extent far greater than the three places included in its title. It provided the main line from Madrid via Zaragoza to Barcelona; it had a main line running south-eastwards from Madrid to Alicante and it ran south and south-westwards to Cordoba and Seville, and provided the main line between Madrid and Lisbon, attaining practically to the Portuguese frontier at Badajoz. The engine illustrated was one of a large class of German-built four-cylinder compounds, of which the first were introduced in 1901. They proved excellent engines, and the original thirty of 1901–3 were followed by a further seventy-five added to the stock between the years 1905 and 1913. They were built in various batches by several of the well-known German manufacturers, including Hanomag, Henschel, and Maffei. It is only now, after more than sixty years of service for the majority of them, that they are being taken out of traffic. The cylinder diameters were: $14\frac{3}{4}$ in. high pressure; $21\frac{1}{2}$ in. low pressure, with a common stroke of $25\frac{1}{2}$ in. The original engines of 1901 had an 'all-up' weight of 102 tons with their tenders, while the later ones, though having the same boilers and machinery were slightly heavier.

74 **Andalusian Railway**: Four-cylinder Compound 4-6-0 of 1902.

The former Andalusian Railway, the 'Andaluces', was unlike most of the other pre-nationalization railways of Spain in that it operated in a fairly compact area, south of the Madrid, Zaragoza, and Alicante main line, running through Cordoba and Seville to the coast at Huelva. The Andaluces served Cadiz, Algeciras, Malaga, Granada, and Almeria. Its principal contacts with one of the larger Spanish railways were almost entirely those with the Madrid, Zaragoza, and Alicante, and the success of the four-cylinder compounds on the latter line (ref. 73) may have influenced the Andaluces. The engine illustrated has a strikingly French appearance, and is actually a de Glehn compound, with faithful representations of the French type of boiler mountings and bogie, but a most curious little four-wheeled tender. Their cylinder dimensions were the same as those of the German-built Madrid, Zaragoza, and Alicante engines, but the coupled wheels were smaller, 5 ft. $3\frac{3}{4}$ in. against 5 ft. $8\frac{1}{2}$ in. The first batch of ten was built in 1902 by the Société Usine de Graffenstaden in France, and these remained the only ones in service until 1928. Then it was a remarkable tribute to the original design that a further twenty-two identical engines were added, but in this latter case by Spanish builders in Bilbao—seventeen by Babcock & Wilcox, and five by Euskalduna. Many of these handsome little engines are still at work today.

75 **London and North Western Railway:** The 'Precursor'.

Reference has been made under Plates 1 and 2 to the Webb compounds of the London and North Western Railway. After his retirement more powerful engines were urgently needed, and his successor, George Whale, reverted to the simplest type of express passenger locomotive, the inside cylinder 4-4-0. One hundred and thirty of these compact, and very reliable, engines were turned out at Crewe Works in the years 1904–7, and they are exceptionally interesting not only for their detail engineering features, but for their altogether contrasting appearance to some Continental locomotives of the same period, which not only had appurtances hung on at many places outside, but which had all the piping arranged externally. The 'Precursors' had cylinders 19 in. diameter by 26 in. stroke; coupled wheels 6 ft. 9 in. diameter, and a large boiler with a heating surface of 2009 sq. ft. By Continental standards the grate area of the firebox, $22\frac{1}{2}$ sq. ft., would be considered very small for a heavy main line engine of the day; but the 'Precursors' were fired with high-grade coal, Welsh, or Yorkshire hards, and steamed very freely. They hauled trains of 350 to 400 tons at average speeds of 55 m.p.h., taking such loads about 65 m.p.h. on level track. All the class were named, mostly after previous London and North Western Railway engines, on which the names were handed down from one generation of Crewe products to the next.

76 **Eastern Railway of France:** 4-4-0 Non-compound Passenger Locomotive.

One's first impression of this remarkable engine is of the strange contrast its complicated exterior presents to the London and North Western 'Precursor' 4-4-0 on the same page, to which it is very similar in tractive power, having two cylinders 18½ in. diameter by 26 in. stroke. So far as the engine proper is concerned the outside cylinders drive the rear pair of coupled wheels, and the valve gear is the ordinary Stephenson link motion which with its eccentrics and links looks very complicated when arranged outside. The peculiar boiler was an invention of Flaman. The lower barrel was completely full of fire tubes, and the upper cylinders provided the steam space. The boiler was a large one by French standards of the day providing 1800 sq. ft. of heating surface—though not so much as the simple, orthodox type used on the 'Precursor', which had over 2000 sq. ft. Speeds on the Est were not high in those years, rarely exceeding 60 m.p.h., and a particular performance by one of these engines gave a start-to-stop average speed of 41 m.p.h. over the 58½ miles from Troyes to Chaumont. One must not make direct comparisons with contemporary English speeds, except to say that the French engines did their work with great ease and economy.

77 **Caledonian Railway:** The Dunalastair IV Class.

On Plate 17 of this book is depicted the second variety of the famous Caledonian 'Dunalastair' family of locomotives of which five were purchased by the Belgian Government and put to work on the most important expresses. A subsequent development of these notable engines in Belgium is illustrated later in this book. The picture referred to above shows a later development on the Caledonian Railway itself, which originated in 1904. In that year the fourth 'Dunalastair' series was introduced, with still larger boilers, and higher pressure. These engines did remarkable work on the sharply timed special postal trains. They conveyed heavy loads, and achieved the same record of reliability as the earlier and smaller 'Dunalastair' engines. The final development, illustrated here but slightly beyond the general period of this book was the superheated version introduced in 1910. With these latter engines equally fast and powerful as the earlier 'Dunalastair IV' class, some striking economies in coal consumption were achieved. On the long night runs from Perth to Carlisle and back, 300 miles in all, it was necessary to re-coal at Carlisle with the non-superheater engines. With the superheater engines one tender-full was enough for the complete night's work in heavy and fast express duty.

78 **Paris–Orléans Railway:** Four-cylinder de Glehn Compound 4-4-0.

The Paris–Orléans Railway followed the Nord very closely in its locomotive practice, introducing 4-4-0 and later 4-4-2 compound express engines (ref. 103) of similar, but slightly larger, dimensions, benefiting from the experience of their friends and allies in the north. Running conditions on the Orléans were, however, rather different, in that the line includes some very long stretches of straight, almost dead level track, and in the early 1900s the speed was limited to 100 km.p.h. (62½ m.p.h.) over long stretches. Express train loads on the Orléans, particularly those of the crack service that were most sharply timed, were not heavy, rarely exceeding 200 tons. Typical runs of the early 1900s were: Bordeaux to Angoulême, 87 miles in 95 minutes; Angoulême to Poitiers, 70½ miles in 80 minutes; and Poitiers to St Pierre des Corps, 63 miles in

69 minutes. The Orléans engines did their work with quiet efficiency, and are important in view of the gradual development of the French locomotive that took place in the late 1920s under André Chapelon. These 4-4-0s provide the earliest starting-point of that development, unlike the Caledonian 'Dunalastair IV' class illustrated on the same page, which marked the culmination of an epoch in locomotive development.

79 **Great Northern Railway, Ireland:** 4-4-0 Express Passenger Engine.

The Great Northern, providing direct communication between twin cities of Dublin and Belfast, always gave an excellent express train service, and the locomotive headquarters was located at the approximate 'half-way house' of the route, at Dundalk. There locomotives, carriages, and wagons were constructed, and it formed also a natural centre for the locomotive running department. In 1900 Charles Clifford, who held the title of Locomotive Superintendent, was also responsible, like his colleagues elsewhere in Ireland, for carriages and wagons. The 4-4-0 locomotive we illustrate was a simple, straightforward design wholly in the British traditions of the period, with 18½ in. by 26 in. cylinders; 6 ft. 7 in. coupled wheels, a total heating surface of 1362 sq. ft., and a working pressure of 175 lb. per sq. in. The colour scheme of green and red-brown under-frames, although reminiscent of the English Great Northern differed in its tones, while distinctive Irish touches were the decorative bead over the driving-wheel splashers, and the name. In other respects, particularly in the use of transfer figures instead of a separate number-plate, the style was definitely like that of the English Great Northern.

80 **Great Northern Railway, Ireland:** Composite Semi-corridor Carriage.

At the turn of the century there was still considerable reluctance among railway managements to introduce full corridor trains on account of the reduced seating accommodation they afforded for every ton of dead-weight to be hauled. At the same time dining-cars were demanded by the more affluent of passengers. For some little time a compromise was made by having part of the train vestibuled, and the coach illustrated was one of a three-car set run on the Dublin–Belfast expresses. The set consisted of one first and second composite carriage; one second and third composite as illustrated in our picture; and between these two was the dining-car. These cars were relatively short, even by the standards of 1900, being only 52 ft. long; but the interior appointments for all classes were as handsome as the exterior finish. The rest of the train was made up of non-corridor third-class carriages with semi-elliptical roofs, and including no fewer than ten compartments seating thus 100 passengers. These coaches measured only 51 ft. long, as compared with Churchward's 70 ft. coaches on the Great Western Railway which seated eighty passengers in a corridor coach. The saving in dead-weight in the non-corridor coach was thus appreciable.

81 **Belfast and Northern Counties Railway:** Two-cylinder Compound 4-4-0 Locomotive.

From the year 1876 the locomotive department of this enterprising line was under the superintendency of Mr Bowman Malcolm. He took office at the early age of twenty-two, and remained there after the railway itself was absorbed into the English Midland Railway, and was administered by the Northern Counties Committee. He did not retire until after the Midland Railway itself had become part of the London, Midland and Scottish Railway. Mr Malcolm adopted the two-cylinder Worsdell von Borries system as standard from 1890. His earliest engines of this type were 2-4-0s, and in 1901 he brought out his so-called 'heavy compounds', to distinguish them from the earlier 'light compounds'. The 'heavy compound' which is the subject of our picture, was the standard passenger engine of the line for thirteen years. There were thirteen of them, and two were named *King Edward VII* and *Queen Alexandra*. They had the characteristic slow exhaust resulting from only two beats per revolution, but were in actual fact fast and efficient engines that did excellent work on the Belfast–Londonderry expresses, and the seaside trains to Portrush. Their cylinder diameters were 18 in. high pressure and 26 in. low pressure; the stroke was 24 in., and the coupled wheel diameter was 6 ft. In later years they were rebuilt as two-cylinder simple engines, but the process was not rapid and the last one to remain as a compound No. 63, *Queen Alexandra*, was not rebuilt until 1936.

82 **Belfast and Northern Counties Railway:** Transporter Truck with Narrow Gauge Carriage being Conveyed.

The Belfast and Northern Counties Railway had both broad and narrow gauge sections, and one of Mr Malcolm's two-cylinder compound engines for the Ballymena and Larne section is described under reference 39. The narrow gauge sections were to some extent catered for by a small works at Larne, to which supplies could be taken by sea; but when engines and carriages needed more extensive repair or general overhaul they had to be conveyed to Belfast over broad gauge tracks. Mr Malcolm designed the special transporter for conveyance of narrow gauge stock, and our picture not only illustrates this truck, but also one of the handsome saloon carriages used on the narrow gauge sections. At the time Mr Malcolm was in office the Ballycastle Railway in the north was quite independent, though running in connection with the Belfast and Northern Counties Railway at Ballymoney. Before the end of the nineteenth century the Belfast and Northern Counties Railway had adopted bogie carriages as standard for all new construction, both on the broad and narrow gauge sections. In this connection there was no suburban traffic to provide for, from Belfast, and it was of course for such traffic that many of the English companies continued building non-bogie stock until well into the twentieth century. All Belfast and Northern Counties Railway carriages in our period were lit by compressed-oil gas.

83 **Canadian Pacific Railway:** 4-6-0 Express Locomotive.

The construction of the Canadian Pacific Railway was one of the greatest engineering and sociological events taking place in the British Empire during the nineteenth century, yet from the outset the major influence upon motive power and rolling-stock came from the U.S.A. rather than from Great Britain. Towards the end of 1902, however, an order was placed with Neilson Reid & Co. of Glasgow for thirty-two express passenger 4-6-0s. They were of Canadian design and incorporated many American features, including a steeply coned boiler. The valve gear was, however, Stephenson's link motion arranged between the frames. The prototypes of this new design were built at the Canadian

Pacific Railway works in Montreal. They were interesting as having the sandboxes below the boiler barrel. They were very powerful engines for their period, having cylinders 20 in. diameter by 26 in. stroke, the coupled wheels were 5 ft. 9 in. diameter, and the nominal tractive effort no less than 27,100 lb. A remarkable feature of these engines, which contributed to their free running and generally excellent performance, was the size of the piston valves. When British engines with comparable cylinder dimensions had valves of 8 in. or 9 in. diameter, these Canadian engines had valves of no less than 12 in. diameter. The weight of the engine alone was $82\frac{1}{2}$ tons.

84 **Canadian Pacific Railway:** Observation Car.

The Canadian Pacific Railway cuts through the Rocky Mountains amidst scenery of almost unexampled magnificence, and from the outset the company sought to capitalize this asset by providing special observation cars with open platforms at the rear at the tail-end of the principal transcontinental trains. These open-ended cars were ideal for summer conditions, but the winters are exceptionally severe, and so to be in a position to provide the observation car facility all the year round the enterprising management introduced some special cars for winter use, one of which is illustrated in our picture. The central portion of the car formed an observation saloon, with revolving chairs, to accommodate fourteen passengers. At each end was a raised portion, in which there were six revolving chairs. This idea was the forerunner of the modern vista-dome, incorporated in certain American express trains. and also on the Rheingold express in Germany. This Canadian car thus provided accommodation for thirty-two sightseers. The journey through the Rockies was always a slow process, while the locomotives—often three to a train—were labouring up tremendous gradients like the celebrated Field Hill. But with these fine observation cars the run through the mountains could be exhilarating rather than tedious.

85 **Union Pacific Railroad:** 4-6-0 Express Passenger Locomotive.

The Union Pacific, one of the best known of all American railroads, forms part of one of the most direct routes from Chicago to San Francisco. Its territory begins at Omaha, 501 miles from Chicago, and takes the line over the Rocky Mountains 552 miles farther on at the 'Continental Divide' near Sherman, 8245 ft. above sea-level. One can travel either by the Chicago and North Western or by the Burlington route to reach Omaha; the through 'Limited' train, the Overland Flyer of seventy years ago, was worked over the North Western. From Omaha the Union Pacific used the type of engine shown in our picture for the transcontinental expresses on the section between Omaha and Cheyenne at the foot of the mountain range. They had cylinders 20 in. diameter by 24 in. stroke, and coupled wheels 5 ft. 9 in. diameter. At that time Americans were still using inside valve gear and the practice of hanging innumerable accessories on the outside had scarcely begun. The so-called 'diamond-stack'—all locomotive chimneys or funnels are 'stacks' in the U.S.A.—is an earlier form of spark arrester, used to minimize the effect of fire-throwing with the light, friable lignite of Wyoming used on the Union Pacific. The diamond-stack had a curved screen over the top and a deflector inside for throwing the sparks down. Similar engines, but with coupled wheels, 5 ft. 2 in. diameter, were used on the mountain section, and heavy trains needed two of them.

86 **Chicago and North Western Railroad:** 'Atlantic' Type High Speed 4-4-2 Locomotive.

The Chicago and North Western Railroad had a reputation for high-speed running and reference has already been made in this book 18 to the working of the 'Fast Mail', which ran nightly between Chicago and Omaha. When this was first put on in 1899 it was worked by 4-4-0 locomotives, but the needs of traffic soon demanded something larger, and the fine Atlantic-type engines were later introduced. If one compares the subject of our present illustration with reference 18, it will be seen that there is a strong family likeness though the 4-4-2 has the advantage of much larger boiler and firebox. These engines worked the 'Overland Flyer' between Chicago and Omaha, handing over to the Union Pacific at the latter place. The 'family likeness' was not so much a railway design as a reflection of the standard practice of the builders, Schenectady. At the same time they were building 4-6-0s for the New York Central, which had exactly the same characteristic features. These latter had on their tenders one of the longest collection of initials I have ever known, namely N.Y.C. & H.R.R.R. The second part included the Hudson River part of the railroad's full name. For an American railroad, even in those days, the Chicago and North Western was modest in the way it displayed its initials.

87 **East Indian Railway:** Standard 0-6-0 Goods Engine.

Were it not for the colour and the unusual extent of the cab roof, this neat, highly conventional locomotive would readily pass as an ordinary British goods design. The East Indian, during the time of Mr Rendell's superintendency, was indeed one of the most 'English' of the Indian railways in its locomotive practice, and the symmetry of the designs certainly befitted an engineer who had been trained on the Brighton under William Stroudley. The engines in question were built by Neilson Reid & Co. of Glasgow, and had cylinders 18 in. diameter by 26 in. stroke; and coupled wheels 5 ft. 1 in. diameter. They were no more than moderate powered machines, and although designed for burning inferior Indian coal had boilers having no more than 1240 sq. ft. of heating surface. The grate area was 24 sq. ft.—above the average for contemporary British locomotives of equivalent tractive power. The working pressure was only 160 lb. per sq. in. Like 0-6-0 engines in England at the time these engines were used on intermediate passenger trains when necessary, and were fitted with the automatic vacuum brake. As in British practice the sandboxes were accommodated on the running-plate, and incorporated in the splashers for the leading pair of coupled wheels.

88 **N.G.S.R., India:** 4-6-0 Express Locomotive.

The above initials are an abbreviation of the full title of this one-time privately owned railway in India: His Exalted Highness the Nizam's Guaranteed State Railway, running in the State of Hyderabad. This railway which at the turn of the century operated some 350 miles of line on the 5 ft. 6 in. Indian broad gauge, and also about 400 miles of metre gauge track, provided a through-express train service between Hyderabad and the port of

Bombay. Speeds in India were then nowhere high, and these 4-6-0 locomotives had smaller wheels than most then engaged in main line passenger service. Power to climb the intermediate gradients was needed, and the cylinders were 18 in. by 26 in. stroke, in combination with 5 ft. diameter driving wheels. The engines of this class, built by Dübs & Co. of Glasgow, were typical of what may be termed the Anglo-Indian style, clearly showing evidence of British influence in the neatness of outline, and absence of external pipes and gadgets, but at the same time not conforming to any particular style on the home railways, nor to the 'house-style' of any of the well-known manufacturers. Necessary features for the Indian working were the large canopied cab, and the extensive cowcatcher.

89 **Paris–Orléans Railway:** 4-6-0 Mixed Traffic Locomotive.

In this grade of service, as in express passenger motive power, the Paris–Orléans and the Northern railways moved forward in close collaboration with each other. Neither used the 4-6-0 as a standard express type, and passed from the 4-4-0 to the 4-4-2, and then at a time a little later than that of the present book, from the 4-4-2 to the 4-6-2. The Paris, Lyons, and Mediterranean, the Est, and the Ouest all used 4-6-0s as their principal express type for a time. The Nord and the Orléans, however, introduced the 4-6-0 as a medium-powered mixed-traffic engine and our picture shows the Orléans variety, which had its almost exact counterpart on the Nord. They were de Glehn four-cylinder compounds, and had all the usual contemporary features of that type. They were used for both intermediate passenger and fast goods traffic, and a number were in service until quite recently. The cylinder diameters were 14 in. high pressure and 22 in. low pressure, both with a stroke of $25\frac{1}{4}$ in. The boiler was an excellent one with 2093 sq. ft. of heating surface and a grate area of $26\frac{1}{2}$ sq. ft. The coupled wheels were 5 ft. 9 in. diameter but this was no detriment to fast running, and they have worked easily and comfortably at speeds of 70 m.p.h. They were altogether extremely useful engines.

90 **Midland Railway:** American-built 2-6-0 Goods Engine.

Reference has already been made in connection with Plate 22 to the locomotive 'famine' that affected several English railways at the turn of the century. The Midland purchased no fewer than forty from the U.S.A., and as one manufacturer could not supply them all in the short time specified the order was divided: thirty to Baldwins and ten to Schenectady. The Baldwin batch were almost identical in general design to those supplied to the Great Northern (ref. 22) except that the Midland ones had the sandboxes on the top of the boiler, American fashion. The Schenectady batch, as illustrated under this reference, had a much more English appearance, except of course for the very large cab. These engines were further distinguished from the Baldwins by having standard Midland six-wheeled tenders. It is of interest to recall, however, that the double-bogie tenders common to the Baldwin 2-6-0s on both the Great Northern and the Midland had a lighter unloaded weight than the English six-wheelers, due to thinner plates and a generally lighter construction. This, of course, explains why they did not last so long. The Midland 2-6-0s were used on the coal trains. Ten each of the Baldwins were originally stationed at Leeds, Sheffield, and Toton yards, near Nottingham. The ten Schenectadys were originally at Wellingborough.

91 **Wellington and Manawatu Railway, New Zealand:** 4-6-0 Passenger Engine of 1904.

The early history of railways in New Zealand was one of curiously disjointed individual efforts, some by private companies and others by the State. There was the same divergence of view on the rail gauge. One of the most important and successful of the early railways was the privately projected Wellington and Manawatu, which came to form part of the North Island trunk main line between Wellington and Auckland. The Manawatu line was no more than 84 miles in length, but it remained independent until 1908 when all the former privately-owned railways were taken over by the Government. The Manawatu imported some excellent and thoroughly characteristic American locomotives from Baldwins, and our first picture illustrates one of the passenger 4-6-0s introduced in 1904. Running on the 3 ft. 6 in. gauge eventually standardized throughout New Zealand they were not large engines, having cylinders $16\frac{1}{2}$ in. diameter by 22 in. stroke; coupled wheels 4 ft. 10 in. diameter, and a nominal tractive effort of 15, 280 lb. The weight of the engine alone was $39\frac{1}{2}$ tons, and $66\frac{3}{4}$ tons with its eight-wheeled bogie tender. In New Zealand they were usually known by the American term for the type, 'ten-wheeler', rather than the simple English '4-6-0'. They had relatively small boilers with a total heating surface of only 1089 sq. ft., and a grate area of 16.1 sq. ft. They were successful and long-lived engines, later known as the New Zealand Government Railways Class 'Ud'.

92 **New Zealand Government Railways:** The 41 ft. 'Birdcage' Saloon Carriage.

The New Zealand Government Railways, having established a well-equipped carriage works at Addington, Christchurch, proceeded to develop a distinctly original form of carriage design, which was something of a compromise between the compartment stock of the British home railways and the open saloons of America. The compromise resulted in the rather curious type of carriage shown in our picture, one built at Addington in 1895. The left-hand end, as seen in the picture, provided a large open saloon with chair-type seats like a modern lounge car. There was a lavatory in the centre and two small compartments at the right-hand end. Why the gangway giving access to these separate compartments had to be open one cannot say; but the type proved popular with first-class passengers, and quite a number were built. Furthermore they had a long life, and after the Second World War a number of them had been derated to second class. In the course of time, however, no one seems to have thought of closing in that open 'bird-cage' gangway. Imagine going outside on a freezing cold winter's night while the train was bowling along at 40 to 50 m.p.h.! They were very lightly constructed and weighed only 15 tons tare.

93 **Wellington and Manawatu Railway:** 2-8-4 Passenger Tank Engine.

The Manawatu line was a railway of striking contrasts. Thirty-five miles north of Wellington is the notorious Rimutaka incline where the gradient is 1 in 15 for 3 miles. This incline is equipped for rack working on the Fell system, and with heavy trains as many as four of the special 'rack' tank engines were needed. The tank engine illustrated is of conventional type. Again it is a thoroughgoing American design, with bar frames, twin sandboxes on the top of the boiler, and a very airy and commodious cab. This class of locomotive was introduced for the shorter distance traffic around Wellington. It later became a New Zealand railway standard of Class 'Wj'. They had cylinders 17 in. diameter by 20 in. stroke; coupled wheels 3 ft. 7 in. diameter, and the usual rather small New Zealand boiler of the day, with 1076 sq. ft. of heating surface, and a grate area of 16.7 sq. ft. In commenting upon the size of New Zealand locomotives, however, I must relate this to the low maximum axle load permitted, and these 2-8-4 tanks had a maximum of only 10 tons. Nevertheless with such small coupled wheels and the high boiler pressure of 200 lb. per sq. in. the nominal tractive effort was 21,510 lb. Like the 4-6-0s of the New Zealand Government Railways Class 'Ud', these 2-8-4s, were built by Baldwins in 1904.

94 **Wellington and Manawatu Railway:** 2-8-0 Compound Freight Engine.

Reference has been made in many parts of this book to the vogue for compound locomotives that swept over Europe and the U.S.A. at the turn of the century. Europe favoured the de Glehn, the von Borries, and the Gölsdorf systems, while in the U.S.A. the systems of Vauclain and that of the 'tandem' for a time predominated. In England the Webb compound system used so extensively at one time on the London and North Western Railway was largely discredited by the year 1901. The Manawatu 2-8-0 illustrated is of particular interest. It was built in 1896 and was the first Vauclain compound for service outside the U.S.A. In the Vauclain compound the high and low pressure cylinders are arranged in two pairs, with the high pressure and low pressure on each side of the locomotive driving a common crosshead. But although all four cylinders were outside the valve gear was inside; so also were the valves, in what must have been a very inaccessible position. The cylinder diameters were 11 in. high pressure and 18 in. low pressure with a stroke of 20 in. The coupled wheel diameter was 3 ft. 7 in. and the boiler pressure 180 lb. per sq. in. Nominal tractive effort of these engines was 13,600 lb. Later they became the New Zealand Government Railways Class 'Oa'.

95 **'Big Four':** 'Atlantic' type Express Passenger Locomotive.

The 'Big Four' cities whose names are embodied in the title of this important railway are Cleveland, Cincinnati, Chicago, and St Louis. In studying the comparative dimensions of contemporary British and American locomotives the point that immediately strikes one in the majority of American designs is the huge size of the boilers and fireboxes. The cylinders were not unusually large, compared for example with the largest British engines, like the North Eastern 'V' class Atlantic (ref. 105), or the Caledonian 4-6-0 No. 50 (ref. 175) But taking the 'Big Four' Atlantic as typical, the total heating surface was 3340 sq. ft. and the grate area was no less than 51.7 sq. ft.—the latter roughly *double* the average size of contemporary large British locomotives of the day. Generally speaking the coal was of much poorer quality than that normally used in Great Britain, and it was also customary to thrash engines much more vigorously, resulting in a high coal consumption. It goes almost without saying that the running-plate is carried high above the coupled wheels, leaving everything exposed, except the valve gear which is between the frames. This impressive engine, which weighed 83 tons without its tender, was built by the American Locomotive Company of New York.

96 **Canadian Northern Railway:** 4-6-0 Passenger Locomotive.

This line, like the Grand Trunk referred to under 97, was built up by a series of amalgamations, and in its central area at Winnipeg it was very much interlaced with the Canadian Pacific. One of its most important eastern terminals was at Port Arthur on Lake Superior, and from Winnipeg its main line ran north-westwards at first to Edmonton, and then at a time later than that of this book a highly competitive route was constructed through the Rockies by the Yellowhead Pass, to run southwards and eventually parallel to the Canadian Pacific main line on the opposite side of the Fraser River canyon. The effects of this competition are outside our period, but mention of it is enough to show that the Canadian Northern was a highly enterprising line. The locomotive chosen for illustration is like its rivals of the Canadian Pacific (ref. 83) and the Grand Trunk (ref. 97) of the 4-6-0 type, though of somewhat smaller proportions. The cylinders were 18 in. diameter by 24 in. stroke; the coupled wheels were 5 ft. 3 in. diameter; the total heating surface 1865 sq. ft. and the grate area 29.2 sq. ft. Like all three Canadian engines the boiler barrel is slightly tapered.

97 **Grand Trunk Railroad, Canada:** 4-6-0 Express Passenger Locomotive.

This great line, second only in fame to the Canadian Pacific in the early 1900s, incorporated the oldest railway in Canada, opened in 1836 between St Johns, Quebec, and La Prairie. The Grand Trunk itself was projected in 1853, and was intended to be a main trunk line of railway throughout Canada. It was originally constructed on the 5 ft. 6 in. gauge, but was converted to standard gauge in 1873–4. The Grand Trunk did not confine its operations to Canada, and one of its most important routes led into the U.S.A. crossing the Niagara rapids, within sight of the famous falls to reach Buffalo. One of its best-known trains was 'the International Limited' running between Chicago and Montreal. The 4-6-0 locomotive illustrated, another product of the American Locomotive Company, was like so many North American engines of the day in being more characteristic of its builders than of its owners. Like the 'Big Four' Atlantic described under reference 95, it had a large boiler and firebox in relation to cylinder volume, though only in relation to contemporary British practice. The cylinders were 20 in. diameter by 26 in. stroke, and against these dimensions the total heating surface was 2415 sq. ft. and the grate area 33.4 sq. ft. The boiler pressure was unusually high for North America at that time, 225 lb. per sq. in.

98 **Central Railroad of New Jersey:** 4-6-0 Built 1902 and Subsequently Superheated.

This railway had a main line extending over 191 miles from Jersey City to Scranton, and at the turn of the century practically all its locomotives were characterized by wide fireboxes of the Wootten type and cabs astride the boiler in the 'Mother Hubbard' style. The class of engine shown in our picture is a modernized but not beautiful version of a 4-6-0 introduced in

1902 for heavy local and suburban express service out of the western suburbs of New York. The trains consisted of heavy clerestory-roofed all-steel stock and required a high tractive effort in starting away. These engines in consequence had coupled wheels only 5 ft. 9 in. diameter. Originally they had 19 in. by 26 in. cylinders and slide valves actuated by Stephenson link motion inside. As rebuilt they had 20 in. by 26 in. cylinders, piston valves, and Walschaerts gear. The grate area, as usual with American locomotives having the Wootton firebox, was enormous, 67.7 sq. ft. Unlike many 'Mother Hubbard'-type American engines those of the Central of New Jersey had quite reasonable shelter for the fireman, and these 4-6-0s, both in their original and rebuilt form had a full 'cab'. It was a great sight to see the evening commuter trains, one after another, thundering out of Jersey City Terminal behind these engines.

99 **Great Northern Railway:** The Pioneer British 'Atlantic' Engine.

The veteran Great Northern Railway Locomotive Superintendent, Patrick Stirling, died in office in 1895, and he was succeeded by Henry A. Ivatt. The new chief was not long in completely reversing his predecessor's design practice by providing locomotives with large boiler capacity and moderate cylinder volume. After building some 4-4-0s, Ivatt astonished the British locomotive world by the production of the first engine of the 'Atlantic' (4-4-2) type to run in this country. As illustrated elsewhere in this volume there were already engines of this type running in the U.S.A. The Great Northern engine No. 990 was introduced in 1898, the year of the celebrated 'gold rush', and the class of which it was the pioneer were nicknamed the 'Klondykes'. Actually the engine No. 990 was named *Henry Oakley* after the General Manager who had just retired and been appointed to the Board. It remained the only named Great Northern engine until 1922, when the first of the Gresley Pacifics was completed at Doncaster works. The engine 990 had relatively small cylinders, 18 in. diameter by 24 in. stroke, but a very large boiler. The class proved excellent in traffic, but from 1902 onwards their work was rather overshadowed by the achievements of the still larger boilered variety, illustrated in Plate 139.

100 **Atlantic City Railroad:** Vauclain Compound Express 4-4-2.

In the successful development of the 'Atlantic' type in the U.S.A. there was no more spectacular example than these striking engines used on the Atlantic City 'flyers'. They were of the 'Mother Hubbard' category, with the driver's cab arranged half-way along the boiler, and with the fireman on his own at the back of the huge Wootten firebox. The Vauclain compound system provided for the two pairs of cylinders—one high pressure and one low pressure to be mounted one on each side of the engine, and the pistons from each pair were coupled together to drive a common connecting-rod from one 'small-end'. These engines were designed for high-speed running and had coupled wheels of 7 ft. diameter. The cylinder diameters were 13 in. high pressure and 22 in. low pressure with a common stroke of 26 in. The total heating surface was 1835 sq. ft., and the grate had the enormous area of 76 sq. ft. The boiler pressure was 200 lb. per sq. in. These engines frequently attained speeds of over 80 m.p.h. and their exploits became the subject of certain legends as feats of speed tended to become exaggerated. From all accounts they rode well at high speeds though one fears the driver would not feel so comfortable perched up on the frames as he would in a cab of the orthodox kind, working in close collaboration with his fireman.

101 **Northern Railway of France:** de Glehn Compound 'Atlantic'.

It would not be an exaggeration to state that these locomotives, first introduced in 1900, are one of the famous classes ever to run anywhere in the world. The system of compounding devised by the English engineer Alfred de Glehn was adopted by Monsieur du Bousquet, of the Nord, in 4-4-0 locomotives; but it was in the Atlantics, running the English boat trains between Paris and Boulogne and Calais that the performance of the de Glehn compounds attracted world-wide attention. One of the most famous developments was on the English Great Western Railway, while the de Glehn system was adopted in Switzerland, in Germany to a limited extent, and in Spain. Engines that were the precise equivalent of the Nord 'Atlantics' were built for Egypt, while in India the Bengal Nagpur Railway introduced Atlantics, and some years later Pacifics working on the same system. The high pressure cylinders are outside, driving the rear pair of coupled wheels, while the low pressure are inside, and driving the leading pair. Although the Nord subsequently built many very fine Pacifics, the Atlantics of 1900–3 vintage were still being called upon for first-class express passenger service more than thirty years later. The photograph on which our picture was based was taken at La Chapelle depot, Paris, in 1934 when the locomotive in question was about to take an express to Lille.

102 **Great Western Railway:** de Glehn Compound 4-4-2 No. 103 *President.*

The early years of the twentieth century were a time of much experimenting with compound locomotives, and the very fine performances of the Atlantic engines on the Northern Railway of France, Plate 101, attracted a great deal of attention, On the Great Western, a similar engine, the *La France,* was imported in 1903, and to carry the examination of the de Glehn principle still further two additional engines were purchased in 1904–5, corresponding to an enlarged French design then working on the Paris–Orléans Railway. These two engines, No. 103 *President* and 104 *Alliance,* did some very fine work on the Great Western Railway, but having regard to the extra complication of compounding, and the remarkable work of the Swindon-designed simple engines no further compounds were built for the Great Western Railway. Nevertheless the de Glehn experimental had two very lasting effects which extended to the last days of steam on British railways. That very important engine detail, the 'big-end', was adapted to British requirements and became standard for inside cylinder connecting-rods on the Great Western four-cylinder engines, and later on the London, Midland, and Scottish Railway. It was later applied to the inside cylinder connecting-rods of certain London and North Eastern Railway engines. The de Glehn bogie became also a Great Western, and ultimately a London, Midland and Scottish Railway, standard.

103 **Paris–Orléans Railway:** de Glehn 'Atlantic'.

Under reference 101 emphasis has been laid on the epoch-marking character of the four-cylinder compound 'Atlantic' of the Northern Railway of France. The Orléans engines, which date from 1903, were, in round terms, about 10 per cent larger and had the following leading dimensions: cylinder diameters, high pressure $14\frac{3}{16}$ in. and low pressure $23\frac{5}{8}$ in., with a common stroke of $25\frac{3}{16}$ in. These 'odd' dimensions are, of course, the English equivalent of the exact metric dimensions on the French engines. The boiler was very large, with a total heating surface of 2617 sq. ft. and a grate area of 33.9 sq. ft. The coupled wheel diameter was 6 ft. $8\frac{1}{4}$ in. These engines were designed for working over all sections of the main line between Paris and Bordeaux. Speeds were not then so high on the Orléans as on the Nord, but on tests the larger 4-4-2s gave ample evidence of their quality. They were found capable of hauling trains of 350 tons at 70 m.p.h. on level track. It was this enhanced performance that led G. J. Churchward, of the English Great Western Railway, to purchase two more de Glehn compounds for extended trial in England, and the Great Western Railway engine No. 103 *President* illustrated in connection with figure 102 was one of these. Apart from superficial detail, *President* and the Paris–Orléans 'Atlantic' are identical.

104 **Dutch State Railway:** 'Atlantic' type Express Locomotive.

It is remarkable to recall that by the close of the nineteenth century there were no fewer than five main line railways operating in Holland, and that there was strong competition between two of them for the mail traffic from England conveyed through Holland to Germany. The State company ran in connection with the cross-Channel packets working from Flushing, while the Dutch Rhenish Company ran the boat train from the Hook of Holland. It was to meet competition from the Rhenish Company that the State Railway introduced the very handsome Atlantics shown in our picture. They were a natural development of the 4-4-0 (ref. 16) and like these latter they were built in Manchester by Beyer, Peacock & Co. The Atlantics had cylinders 19 in. diameter by 26 in. stroke; the coupled wheels, 7 ft. diameter, were designed for fast running, while the Belpaire firebox had the very large grate area for that period—particularly with a long narrow grate—of 31 sq. ft. These engines worked the mail trains over the 130 miles between Flushing and the German frontier at Venlo, and over the level, though very exposed section of 48 miles between Flushing and Roosendaal, they averaged 55 m.p.h.

105 **North Eastern Railway:** 'V' class 'Atlantic'.

On Plate 100 there is illustrated one of the celebrated 'Atlantic' engines used in working the fast trains run between Philadelphia and Atlantic City, about which so many legends of exceptionally fast running had grown up. In 1901 a party of railway officers from the North Eastern, headed by that most dynamic of General Managers, George S. Gibb, visited the U.S.A. and duly travelled on one of the Atlantic City 'flyers'. The Locomotive Superintendent, Wilson Worsdell, was very impressed with the working of the American 'Atlantics', and designed one of his own, for the heaviest Anglo-Scottish express services. Nevertheless, while the inspiration is said to have come from America, the contrast in external appearance between the 'Mother Hubbard' and the neat, compact British engine could not have been greater. On the North Eastern the 'V' class engines with their large boilers and generally massive construction proved fast and reliable, though rather heavy on coal when pressed to a high rate of steaming. Despite this they were well liked in the running department, and the majority of the engines of the class had a life of more than forty years. In appearance, with their grace of outline and magnificent finish they were among the most impressive of all British Atlantics.

106 **Baden State Railways:** Four-cylinder Compound 'Atlantic'.

In outward appearance one could not find a much greater contrast than between the very neat, compact, yet massive North Eastern 'Atlantic' constructed at Gateshead Works, and the German compound 'Atlantic' illustrated herewith. Both were close contemporaries, the Baden type having been built by Maffei of Munich in 1902. They had that Maffei speciality of all four cylinders driving on to one axle. This eliminated the effect of hammer blow, made the engines easy on the track and very smooth riding. The cylinders were 13.2 in. diameter high pressure and 22.4 in. low pressure, both with a stroke of 24.4 in. boiler was huge for the period, having a total heating surface of 2550 sq. ft., and the grate area was 42 sq. ft. These engines were designed to haul 200-ton trains at 75 m.p.h. on level track. The section of line over which they operated was between Mannheim and Oldenburg. In service they did very good work, and experienced observers of locomotive performance considered they were the most powerful locomotives outside America. The coupled wheels were very large, 6 ft. 10 in. diameter, and no doubt contributed to the speed-worthiness of the engines.

107 **Shantung Railway, China:** 4-6-0 Passenger Locomotive.

In the early years of the present century the railways of China were greatly developed, largely under European influence, and the engine illustrated is one of a series built by the Saxon Locomotive Works of Chemnitz. Apart from the cow-catcher and the venetian blinds to the cab windows, it is of characteristically German design. It is a two-cylinder simple, non-superheated, with balanced slide valves actuated by the Heusinger gear. The cylinders were 19¾ in. diameter by 24¾ in. stroke; the coupled wheels of no more than 4 ft. 5 in. diameter reflect the hard work on heavy gradients for which these engines were designed, and this was provided for by an excellent boiler having 1907.7 sq. ft. of heating surface with 24¾ sq. ft. of grate area. The boiler pressure was 205 lb. per sq. in. External features to be noted are the sand-box on top of the boiler; the air brake pump arranged horizontally, and special arrangement in the roof of the cab to provide good ventilation. The tender, though apparently not large, carried no less than 8 tons of coal, though the tanks had a capacity of only 2700 gallons. This locomotive provides an interesting contrast to the British-designed engines operating elsewhere in China at about the same time.

108 **Shanghai–Nanking Railway:** 4-6-2 Passenger Tank Engine.

The Shanghai–Nanking Railway was a creation of the twentieth century, and its origin was described in connection with its highly original coat of arms (ref. 63). The locomotives were all built specially, and were of thoroughly modern design for the period. The original passenger engines were of the 4-4-0 type, with outside cylinders, though these were soon afterwards supplemented by the remarkable 4-2-2 engines (ref. 109). For local passenger workings the handsome 4-6-2 tanks illustrated in our picture were built by the North British Locomotive Company. Although built by different manufacturers the boilers, cylinders, and motion of both 4-4-0s and 4-6-2 tanks were the same. These in turn were also the same as those used on the standard main line goods engines, which were of the 4-6-0 type. All had outside cylinders, and inside Stephenson's link motion, actuating ordinary D-slide valves. The cylinders in all three classes were 18 in. diameter by 26 in. stroke; the boilers had a total heating surface of 1630 sq. ft. and a grate area of 28 sq. ft. and the boiler pressure was 180 lb. per sq. in. The coupled wheel diameters were 6 ft. 7 in. on the 4-4-0s, and 4 ft. 9 in. on the 4-6-2 tanks illustrated, and on the 4-6-0 goods engines. All were finished in the very attractive green livery.

109 **Shanghai-Nanking Railway:** 4-2-2 'Imperial Yellow' Mail Engine.

This remarkable engine was constructed at a time a little later than the general period of this book, in 1910 in fact; but the 4-2-2 type was so essentially one of the nineteenth century, and the style and finish of the engine themselves belonged verily to a bygone age. The main line out of Shanghai is level and ideally suited to operation with single-wheelers providing loads were not too heavy. The engines were built by Kerr, Stuart & Co. of Stoke-on-Trent, and immediately became very popular with the Chinese drivers of the day. The finish was superb in 'Imperial yellow', lined out in gold and purple, whereas the ordinary passenger and goods engines of the railway were finished in a medium green, as exemplified by the illustration of the 4-6-2 tank engine (ref. 108). Prior to the introduction of the 'singles' the express trains were worked by a class of outside cylinder 4-4-0s, British built, and of handsome appearance. The 'singles' had cylinders 18 in. diameter by 26 in. stroke; the driving wheels were 7 ft. diameter, and the relatively large boiler had a total heating surafce of 1650 sq. ft. and a grate area of 28 sq. ft. This was without much doubt the largest boiler ever seen put on to a British-built single-wheeler. From all accounts these engines did very well, running freely and economically.

110 **Shanghai-Nanking Railway:** Saloon Carriage.

The equipment of this railway included some exceptionally fine examples of British coaching stock practice, and although the particular vehicle illustrated was not normally available for ordinary passengers it was typical of the practice of railway working overseas on British-managed systems. It was designed for the use of railway officers when engaged on inspection and other duties out on the line, and it contained a 'living room', secretarial office, a bedroom, bathroom, and servants' quarters with kitchen. The accommodation for senior officers was magnificently appointed and an outside observation platform was provided, after the fashion of an admiral's stern-walk on an old-time warship. This car was built by the Metropolitan Amalgamated Carriage and Wagon Company. Although of special design, and so luxuriously appointed internally the external finish was generally similar to the splendid main line rolling-stock introduced from the outset on the through express trains. The lower panels were of grained teak, and the upper panels painted yellow. They carried the dragon device, at each end of the car, facing opposite ways, and the initials of the railway intertwined into a neat monogram. In external appearance this sumptuous saloon differed only from ordinary carriages in having an elliptical, as distinct from a clerestory, roof.

111 **Victorian Government Railways:** Clerestory-Roofed Bogie Composite Carriage.

The coaching stock of the Victorian Government Railway was in process of rapid evolution at the turn of the century. Until 1874 the influence had been entirely British, with carriages built both in Great Britain and in Melbourne. In that year bogie saloon carriages of American build were introduced, and thereafter the bogie type came to supersede all others for both main line and suburban working. The coach illustrated was one of a type used on main line trains before the general introduction of corridor stock. The body and high, square-ended clerestory show the British influence, but the bar-framed bogies are generally in the contemporary American style. When corridor coaches were introduced on the Interstate express running between Melbourne and Adelaide some of the earliest carriages were of the same general design, but much longer, and with six-wheeled bogies. Through running between Melbourne and Sydney was not then possible owing to the different gauges standard in the states of Victoria and New South Wales. The crack trains providing the service between the state capitals at this period used to consist of between six and eight of these bogie clerestory carriages.

112 **Victorian Government Railways:** 4-4-0 Express Passenger Engine 'New A' Class.

Until the year 1884 the locomotive stock was a heterogeneous collection, many built in Great Britain, some in the U.S.A., and a number by the Phoenix Foundry in Ballarat. In 1884 the first step towards Victorian standard designs were taken by the introduction of the so-called 'Old A' class 4-4-0s, built by Beyer, Peacock & Co. in Manchester. They were thoroughly British in appearance, except that the cabs were much larger than anything then customary in England. Five years later came the 'New A' class, which is the subject of our picture. These fine engines became a standard passenger type, and continued to do good work after the introduction of much larger engines. The painting style was elaborate, and contemporary photographs indicate that they were immaculately kept. With the introduction of corridor stock on the long-distance trains they needed assistance on the heavily graded sections. For this the picturesque outside-framed 'B' class 2-4-0s were used, and on double-headed trains it was always the practice to put the most powerful engine in front. The 'New A' class had cylinders 18 in. diameter by 26 in. stroke, coupled wheels 6 ft. diameter, and large boilers providing a total heating surface of 1435 sq. ft. There were 15 engines in this class.

113 **Victorian Government Railways:** 4-6-0 Express Passenger Engine Class 'Dd' of 1904.

Towards the end of our period a considerable change came over the appearance of the locomotive stock. With the need for more powerful engines and the introduction of the 4-6-0 the traditional layout of machinery, with inside cylinders and a low-pitched straight running plate, gave place to the style illustrated in the engine in our picture. A more pronounced change came also in the livery adopted for the entire stud. In the year 1903 Thomas Tait, formerly of the Canadian Pacific Railway, became the new Chairman of Commissioners, in Victoria, and it was at his suggestion that the brilliant array of bright green, brown, and polished brass gave place to the deep maroon style. The colour was similar to the 'Tuscan red' embodied in the Canadian Pacific colour scheme, as shown in the plate (ref. 83). This handsome livery remained standard on the Victorian Railways until about 1920. The 'Dd' class was the forerunner of a series of very successful 4-6-0 engines, which remained the principal express type until 1928, when the first Pacifics were introduced. The 'Dd' class had cylinders 18 in. diameter by 26 in. stroke; coupled wheels 5 ft. $1\frac{1}{2}$ in. diameter and a total heating surface of 1408 sq. ft. and a grate area of $22\frac{1}{2}$ sq. ft. There were eventually 141 engines in this class.

114 **Victorian Government Railways:** Passenger Train Guard's Brake Van.

On the Victorian passenger trains at the end of the nineteenth century luggage compartments were kept entirely separate from the passenger accommodation. There was no equivalent of the popular British carriage with space for luggage at the end of either corridor or non-corridor carriages. The Victorian Railways operated what are termed 'full brakes'. The large bogie van illustrated was of a type used in trains composed of carriages like that illustrated in reference 111. The usual arrangement was to have this van at the rear end of the train. The compartment for the guard himself was relatively small, though very comfortably appointed. The guard's seats, one on each side of the van, were elevated so that he could use the top look-out without standing, and these seats, green upholstered and well padded, sound as though they were more comfortable than some accommodation then provided for passengers! Externally the vertical matchboarding was reminiscent of the standard practice of the Highland Railway in Scotland. The bogies were of the bar-framed type. It will be noted also that Victorian coaches of the period followed the most elaborate English practice in having screw couplings and side chains in addition.

115 **Great Indian Peninsula Railway:** 'Atlantic' type Express Locomotive.

In the early 1900s the 'Atlantic' type enjoyed a lengthy period of popularity in India. On many of the main lines, following the valleys of the great rivers, the gradients were not severe and such did not demand exceptionally high adhesion weight, while the relatively inferior quality of much of the coal made a wide firebox desirable. The Class 'E1' Atlantics introduced on the Great Indian Peninsula Railway by Mr Sarjant were a splendid example of British locomotive construction supplied by the North British Locomotive Co. Ltd. As will be seen from our picture they were large and handsome engines, not unlike the contemporary Robinson 'Atlantics' of the Great Central, but with the standard Great Indian Peninsula Railway stove pipe chimneys and special design of cab. Forty of these engines were built, numbered 900 to 939, and new tradition was established by bestowing upon then names of statesmen prominent in the development of India. These not only included great historical personalities such as *Lord Clive*, *Warren Hastings*, and *Havelock*, but later celebrities, such as the great soldiers of the Empire, *Lord Roberts* and *Lord Kitchener*, and the Viceroy then in office *Lord Curzon*.

116 **Bengal Nagpur Railway:** de Glehn Four-cylinder Compound 'Atlantic'.

The Bengal Nagpur Railway was one of the last Indian lines to remain an entirely privately owned company, and in its locomotive practice it always remained strongly individual. It had two equally important main lines to provide for, one running from Calcutta roughly beside the coast of the Bay of Bengal to make an end-on junction with the Madras Railway at Waltair. The other main line ran westwards across the continent to make an end-on junction with the Great Indian Peninsular Railway at Nagpur. Thus, from Calcutta it formed the first section of great trunk routes to Madras in the first case, and to Bombay in the second. The splendid 'Atlantic' engine illustrated is virtually an Anglo-Indian version of the famous de Glehn 'Atlantics' on the Northern Railway of France (ref. 101) The dimensions of cylinders, coupled wheels, and general proportions are practically identical. The general appearance is, of course, very English, with the addition of louvred windows in the cab and cow-catchers. It is interesting to observe also the use of top-feed to the boiler through the mounting just in front of the dome. This was an important feature of the French compounds that became standard practice of the English Great Western Railway.

117 **East Indian Railway:** Express Passenger 'Atlantic' Locomotive.

This fine engine provides the third example of an Indian Atlantic engine of our period, and in general design it is similar to that of the Great Indian Peninsula Railway, reference 115, with inside Stephenson's link motion, and a very 'English' external style. Despite the level nature of most of its main line however, the East Indian was beginning to experience the need for express passenger engines with greater adhesion weight than that of the 'Atlantics', and at the end of our period some generally similar engines, but of the 4-6-0 type were introduced. As on the G.I.P.R. the Atlantics had boilers with the Belpaire type of firebox, deep and narrow, and the design could be readily adapted to the 4-6-0 type. On the East Indian, 4-4-2s and 4-6-0s alike had cylinders 19 in. diameter by 26 in. stroke; coupled wheels 6 ft. $1\frac{1}{2}$ in. diameter, and boilers with a total heating surface of 1552 sq. ft. and a grate area of 29 sq. ft. The co-existence of 4-4-2 and 4-6-0 designs of similar proportions then had the English parallel on the Great Western and Great Central Railways; but while the 4-4-2 soon gave place to the 4-6-0 at Swindon, the Great Central 'Atlantics' remained in first-class traffic until the mid-1930s.

118 **North Western Railway of India:** Standard 4-4-0 Express Locomotive.

From the port of Karachi the main line of the North Western Railway followed the valley of the Indus to Sukkur, where the line forked. The main line continued in a north-easterly direction to Lahore, while an important branch struck out north-westwards to Quetta. In working the mail trains between Karachi and Lahore the engine workings were divided so that locomotives could be confined to individual drivers, and the section between Karachi and Sukkur was worked by one link with the 4-4-0 type illustrated in our picture. They were excellent engines, of typical nineteenth-century Anglo-Indian design. As a protection to the enginemen tender cabs with louvred windows were an additional refinement. The North Western Railway tended to model itself upon the English North Western, and in 1904 the practice commenced of painting the express locomotives black, with a lining out scheme very similar to that of Crewe. As elsewhere in India at the turn of the century speeds were not high, and much was made of a special run with a Viceregal train when a distance of 52 miles on this route was covered in 64 minutes, with an engine of this class.

119 **Central South African Railways:**
4-6-2 Express Passenger Engines.

At the conclusion of the war, in 1901, urgent attention was given to re-equipping the railways of the Transvaal and the Orange Free State, which were thenceforward operated together as the Central South African Railways. Powerful 4-6-2 passenger engines were supplied by both the Vulcan Foundry and the North British Locomotive Co. Ltd. Our picture illustrates one of the Vulcan engines. It was a very powerful type for the 3 ft. 6 in. gauge at that time, having cylinders 18 in. diameter by 26 in. stroke, coupled wheels 4 ft. 9 in. diameter, and a large boiler having a total heating surface of 1481 sq. ft. The boiler pressure was 200 lb. per sq. in. The engine was equipped for lengthy through runs in country where water supplies at intermediate points were not frequent. The tender was therefore very large having a capacity for 4000 gallons of water and 10 tons of coal. These engines had slide valves placed above the cylinders, actuated by inside Stephenson link motion driving through rocking gear. The similar engines supplied by the North British Locomotive Co. Ltd. also, in 1904, were even larger, with cylinders $18\frac{1}{2}$ in. diameter by 28 in., 5 ft. 2 in. coupled wheels, and a total heating surface of 1842 sq. ft. The North British engines differed from the Vulcans in having Belpaire fireboxes, and piston valves actuated by Walschaerts valve gear. Both were exceptionally fine examples of the British export trade in locomotives.

120 **Central South African Railways:**
4-6-4 Tank Engine.

The independent railways in South Africa in the latter part of the nineteenth century were extensive users of tank engines, even for long main line runs. Under references 153 and 154 will be found descriptions of engines used on the Natal system. Although tender engines were built for the post-war rehabilitation of the Transvaal system for the long through runs, in view of earlier predictions it is not surprising to find some new tank engine designs introduced, and our picture shows a very handsome 4-6-4 built by the Vulcan Foundry late in 1903. The boiler and firebox is the same as that of the 4-6-2 passenger engine (ref. 119), and the cylinders and motion are the same. The coupled wheel diameter is only 4 ft. 6 in., and this in combination with the high boiler pressure of 200 lb. per sq. in. provides a nominal tractive effort of no less than 26,500 lb. Interesting accessories on these engines were the electric headlight, and cow-catchers both front and rear. The water-tanks had a total capacity of 1800 gallons, and the bunker provided space for 3 tons of coal. The total weight in working order of this notable locomotive was 79 tons.

121 **Central South African Railways:** 2-8-2 Heavy Freight Locomotives.

This powerful engine was an almost exact freight counterpart of the North British 4-6-2s mentioned under reference 119. The 4-8-2s had the same design of boiler, with Belpaire firebox. The size of the firebox as seen in our picture is deceptive, for it actually extends a considerable way into the cab, as can be appreciated from a partial blanking off of the cab windows. The firebox provided the large grate area of 33 sq. ft., and was designed for efficient usage of the local coal. Traffic in coal has always been heavy in the Transvaal, and these engines did excellent work with large trains. The building of engines with identical boilers, of the 4-6-2 and 2-8-2 wheel arrangements, for heavy passenger and heavy goods service was an interesting early example of a practice used in the 1920s by Sir Nigel Gresley on the London and North Eastern Railway. A counterpart to his famous Class 'A1' Pacifics was the 2-8-2 design with identical boiler for the Peterborough–London coal traffic. In the English case, however, only two engines of the 2-8-2 type were built. They were too powerful, being capable of handling much heavier trains than the traffic could conveniently deal with. By contrast, the Central South African Railways 2-8-2s became a standard type, and far from being too large were later superseded by very similar, but even larger, engines of the 4-8-2 type.

122 **Z.A.S.M., Transvaal:** 0-6-4 Main Line Tank Engine.

The full title of this principal railway in the former 'South African Republic' was Nederlandsche Zuid Afrikaansche Spoorweg Maatschappij, and the initals were usually abbreviated to Z.A.S.M. This line, before the war, operated some 700 miles of line, and had connections with the Orange Free State Railways and with the British-owned Cape Government Railways. In connection with the latter, before the outbreak of war, a through mail train service was operated between Cape Town and Johannesburg. These were heavy trains consisting of handsome clerestory-roofed bogie stock, and yet in the Transvaal they were hauled by tank engines of the type illustrated in our picture. They had some interesting features of design, including underhung springs on the coupled axles, bar-framed bogies, and outside frames for the coupled wheels. Like all South African trains those of the Transvaal had centre-couplers, and this is shown prominently on the buffer beam. An interesting feature of Z.A.S.M. working was the very elaborate code of headlamps carried on the engines. Our picture shows only three, but it was not unusual to see *five* on the one engine. The engine number was also carried on the chimney, on a special plate, recalling the British use of chimney numbers in the early fifties of the last century. These engines were Dutch built by Messrs. Kessler of Esslingen.

123 **Western Railway of France:** 0-6-0 Suburban Tank Engine.

A first glance at the above illustration might suggest that the title was wrong and that the engine belonged to the English London and North Western Railway. They were actually designed and built in France for suburban duty on the western side of Paris and on the heavily graded sections of the Petit–Ceinture Line (Inner Circle) There are short lengths of 1 in 29, 1 in 67, and 1 in 100 gradients. No less than forty-two engines of this design were built in 1888–9 by the Compagnie de Fives-Lille; but the more one examines their details the more striking becomes the resemblance to the standard practice of Crewe. The suburban carriages of the Parisian lines of that period were however of very light construction, and although these engines were of no more than moderate dimensions they coped admirably with the traffic. The cylinders were 17 in. diameter by $23\frac{1}{2}$ in. stroke; coupled wheels 5 ft. $0\frac{1}{2}$ in. diameter; total heating surface 1071 sq. ft., and grate area 14.7 sq. ft. The sandbox, as customary on most Continental locomotives, was carried on top of the boiler, but in a most unusual and unobtrusive way. The firebox was raised above the line of the boiler barrel, but externally the outer casing of the boiler was continued flush with the top of the outer firebox, and in the space between the outer casing and the boiler barrel was situated the sandbox. This was surely an extreme case of carrying neatness of external appearance to an almost impracticable extent, as the sandbox was broad, long, but very shallow, and must have been very difficult to fill.

124 **Dutch State Railway:** 2-4-0 Passenger Tank Engine.

Although this design belongs to a slightly earlier period than that generally covered by this book, originating in 1877, it is so typical of the products of the British locomotive industry, for export orders that if falls completely into the period. It is, indeed, a locomotive completely in the Beyer, Peacock tradition in all its details: the bell-mouthed chimney; the large, polished brass dome, with its bell-top and the characteristic neatness of outline. Although a locomotive used in humdrum local duties, the class as a whole were a set of most elegant little ornaments, kept spotlessly clean, with their brass and copperwork polished to the utmost extent. They were small in dimensions as well as in their general appearance, with cylinders 16 in. diameter by 24 in. stroke, and coupled wheels 5 ft. 0 in. diameter. The boiler pressure was a modest 135 lb. per sq. in.

125 **Lancashire and Yorkshire Railway:** 2-4-2 Tank Engine of Aspinall Design.

The handsome little engine illustrated was a notable pioneer in more ways than one. It was the first engine to be completed at the new locomotive works of the company at Horwich in 1889, and was in a dual sense a product of the genius of Sir John Aspinall, in his layout of the new workshops, and in his skill as an engine designer. Engine No. 1008, which has been restored to its original condition and is now preserved, was the first of a very large series of 2-4-2 tank engines. Between the introduction of the type, in 1889, and the completion of the final batch of twenty with Belpaire fireboxes and Schmidt superheaters in 1911 no fewer than 330 engines with the 2-4-2 tank wheel arrangement had been constructed, all at Horwich works. The original Aspinall design was developed, stage by stage, to the final version which was so fast-running and economical as to be awarded express passenger rank from the outset. As can be seen from our picture the historic original engine was a very typical, neat, and compact design, with all the 'works' hidden away. As on the London and North Western Railway, the Joy valve gear was standard for many years, and it was used on all the 2-4-2 tank engines. The original series, and nearly all those using saturated steam, had cylinders $17\frac{1}{2}$ in. diameter, with 26 in. stroke. The last twenty, built new with superheaters, had $20\frac{1}{2}$ in.

diameter cylinders, the enlargement being a very accurate representation of the improved on capacity effected in twenty-two years of development of the design.

126 Great Indian Peninsula Railway: 0-6-2 Suburban Tank Engine.

Under the superintendency of Mr Sarjant a general modernization of the Great Indian Peninsula Railway locomotive stock was undertaken, and the programme included the introduction of some powerful new 0-6-2 tank engines for the Bombay suburban services. Even at the turn of the century this traffic was growing rapidly, and in the late 1920s was such as to justify electrification. The passenger trains of the early 1900s weighed about 250 tons tare, and with normal rush-hour loading could easily scale nearly 300 tons gross behind the engine. The new engines, which we illustrate, which were built by Kitson's of Leeds, had cylinders 18 in. diameter by 26 in. stroke; coupled wheels 5 ft. diameter, and the boiler had a total heating surface of 1169 sq. ft. The engine had a large electric headlight. This was not needed in the Bombay surburban area, but it is of considerable historical interest as representing a trial of a new type for eventual use on the large banking engines used for assisting passenger and goods trains on very severe gradients of the Ghat inclines. Apart from the headlight and the cow-catcher the engine had an appearance that is wholly English.

127 Austrian State Railways: The Gölsdorf '170' Class 2-8-0 of 1897.

These famous engines, in some ways the most celebrated of all Karl Gölsdorf's design, were built to handle the through international express passenger trains over the Arlberg Tunnel route. Here the summit level in the 6-mile long tunnel is 4301 ft. and from the west it is approached by a 16-mile bank inclined almost continuously at 1 in 38, commencing at Bludenz. The eastern ascent from Langen in the Tyrol is if anything more severe. The '170' class engines were designed specially for working over the mountain section. They were two-cylinder compounds with all the Gölsdorf specialities, of compound starting valve, double-domes, and the general odd-sided appearance that was inherent in the design. Although originally designed for passenger trains the class was rapidly multiplied and became the standard goods engine for all the State lines. Most of them had a life of more than sixty years, and the photograph from which our picture was prepared was taken in 1964 when the engine in question, together with others of the class, was in steam at Graz, Styria, on the metals of the privately owned Graz–Köflacher Bahn. No finer tribute to the original design could be found than their long life, virtually unchanged from the day they were built.

128 Vienna Metropolitan Railway: Gölsdorf 2-6-2 Compound Tank Engine.

Although this heavily worked line had a management independent of the various main line systems that were operating in Austria some seventy years ago, in engineering matters it followed popular practice of the day, and the engine shown in our picture has all the characteristics of the famous Gölsdorf 4-4-0 express engines, and of his large 2-8-0s designed specially for the Arlberg route. The engine is actually of Gölsdorf design—a two-cylinder compound on his original system. For working in the Metropolitan area, however, where there are a number of tunnels a silencer was provided for the vacuum ejector round the chimney. One of these engines was shown at the Paris Exhibition of 1900, and was given a specially decorative finish. Ordinarily, however, the engines were finished in the same very plain style of the Imperial Royal Austrian State Railways before Gölsdorf visited England and began to adopt rather less gaunt and functional outlines. The Metropolitan tank engines had cylinder diameters of 20½ in. high pressure and 29 in. low pressure, each with a stroke of 25 in. These dimensions gave a capacity for very rapid acceleration from stops, with heavy trains. The coupled wheel diameter was 4 ft. 3 in. Like all Karl Gölsdorf engines, they gave splendid service.

129 **Austrian State Railways:** Gölsdorf 2-6-2 Compound Locomotive.

The locomotives of the Austrian State Railways were some of the most distinctive in Europe. Their designer, Karl Gölsdorf, was one of the most advanced thinkers of the day, and this interesting mixed traffic engine is representative of a change that was gradually taking place from the earlier two-cylinder compound designs with consequently odd-sized cylinders on each side of the engine to the four-cylinder compound type, with the high pressure pair inside, and the low pressure outside. As can be seen from our picture the slide valves placed above the low pressure cylinders were set at an angle. Another distinctive feature was the positioning of the rear carrying wheels at the extreme rear end, presumably to keep the axle-boxes clear of the deep and wide fire box. The boiler barrel was tapered, and in these engines Gölsdorf abandoned the double-dome arrangement. The high pressure cylinders were 14½ in. diameter, and the low pressure 24¾ in., both with a stroke of 28¼ in. The coupled wheels were 5 ft. 11¾ in. diameter, and the large boiler had a total heating surface of 2775 sq. ft. with a grate area of 43 sq. ft. The boiler pressure was 213 lb. per sq. in. The tender was of an unusual design, in which the raised portion on which the number was central had a large oblong opening cover at the top for replenishing the tank. By this much elongated opening it was not necessary precisely to 'spot' the engine when drawing up to a water crane.

130 **Austrian State Railways:** Gölsdorf Four-cylinder Compound 'Atlantic'.

The earliest locomotives designed by Karl Gölsdorf, while ingenious in conception and efficient in service, were highly functional in appearance, of which there is no better example than the Arlberg 2-8-0 illustrated on the opposite page. About this time, however, Gölsdorf paid a visit to England, and was so impressed with the beauty of line and symmetry of appearance of contemporary British locomotives that a considerable change thenceforth came over Austrian locomotives which then became some of the most handsome in Europe. This change also coincided roughly with his change from the two-cylinder to the four-cylinder system of compounding. The removal of pipes and extraneous mountings from the boiler is conspicuous in this compound 'Atlantic', while the use of polished 'blued' steel for the outside boiler cladding gave a most distinguished effect. The cylinder diameters were 14 in. high pressure (outside) and 23¾ in. low pressure, both with a stroke of 26¾ in. The coupled wheel diameter was 7 ft., and the large boiler had a total heating surface of 2248 sq. ft. and a grate area of 38 sq. ft. The coal used was poor, and the high rates of combustion customary on contemporary British locomotives was not possible.

131 Norwegian State Railways: 4-6-0 Compound Goods Engine.

Under reference 107 there is an illustration and description of some 4-6-0 locomotives built for the Shantung Railway in China by the Saxon Locomotive Works of Chemnitz. Our present subject, the Norwegian goods 4-6-0, is another product of the same works and it has some points of family likeness. The Norwegian engine is a two-cylinder compound on the Von Borries system, with outside valve chests and Walschaerts valve gear. The point that immediately strikes one about these engines is the peculiarity of the wheel spacing of both engine and tender. The route for which they were designed is not only very severely graded, but it abounds in sharp curves. Furthermore, their duties involved a good deal of tender-first running. The engine bogie is long, to permit of the large low-pressure cylinder having its centre line horizontal. So far as the tender is concerned, it might have been thought that a six-wheeler would have suffices; but the bogie arrangement used provided the extra flexibility required. A weather plate was fitted on the front of the tender to give protection to the enginemen while running tender first. The cylinder diameters were $17\frac{3}{4}$ in. high pressure and $26\frac{3}{8}$ in. low pressure; the stroke in each case was $25\frac{1}{2}$ in. The coupled wheels were 4 ft. $8\frac{3}{4}$ in. diameter and the total heating surface 1408 sq. ft.

132 Danish State Railways: 4-4-0 Passenger Engine.

Railways in Denmark have to cover relatively short distances and journeys are interrupted by ferry crossings from one island to another. Most of the country is relatively flat, and with shortish runs, level track, and no high speed, the locomotives were of no more than moderate size. The handsome little 4-4-0 illustrated nevertheless includes some interesting features. Designed by Mr Otto Busse, they have what at first sight looks like an unusual and complicated valve gear. It is, however, of English origin, none other than the very efficient Allan straight link motion that gave splendid service on the Highland Railway, and on those famous London and North Western 2-4-0s of the 'Precedent' and 'Whitworth' classes. On all British applications, however, the Allan link motion was inside. The Danish engines were German built by the Hannoversche Maschinenban Actiengesellschaft of Linden. They had 17 in. by 24 in. cylinders—the same size, incidentally, as those of the London and North Western 2-4-0s just mentioned; the coupled wheels were 5 ft. 11 in. diameter, and the boiler had a total heating surface of 1050 sq. ft. and a grate area of 19.2 sq. ft. They were excellent engines in service, and provided yet another example of the saying of an English engineer: 'Who has ever heard of a bad engine with Allan valve gear!'

133 Danish State Railways: 2-4-2 Passenger Tank Engine.

This extremely interesting little engine was a product of the famous German firm of A. Borsig of Berlin-Tegel, notable in being the first and only German firm ever to build locomotives for an English railway. This Danish engine, like the famous South Eastern and Chatham 'L'-class 4-4-0s which Borsig built in 1914, is characteristic of railway rather than of manufacturers' practice. The 2-4-2 type was seen very rarely outside countries of British influence, and this example, with outside cylinders and radial axles is strongly reminiscent of the similar engines built by the Caledonian in Brittain's time for the Callander and Oban line, which also had outside cylinders. The Danish engines also had a Scottish feature in the Allan straight link valve gear; it was arranged outside, and could be studied in its detail as the engine moved about in a station. It is probably not altogether apparent from our picture that the firebox is located between the leading and trailing pair of coupled wheels. Another interesting feature is that the column of the safety valve mounted on the firebox is carried up to a height equal to the top of the cab, so that escaping steam did not obscure the driver's view. The cylinders were 17 in. diameter by 24 in. stroke; coupled wheels 5 ft. 7 in. diameter, and the total weight in working order $51\frac{1}{2}$ tons.

134 **Swedish State Railways:** 2-6-0 Passenger Engine.

The Swedish State Railways had no concern to provide high-speed services, and the maintenance of lines of communications in a largely rural community was the first essential. Gradients were not heavy, but a very high standard of engineering was evident in the soundness of design and excellent workmanship. An outstanding feature that immediately attracted the eye of anyone seeing a Swedish engine for the first time was the 'collar' round the base of the chimney. This was a spark arrester, which was a most important accessory on a railway running through so much forest land where fires started by spark-throwing locomotives could be very serious. These spark arresters, sometimes an inverted funnel form, extended higher up the chimney externally than in the example illustrated. The 2-6-0 in our picture is a very simple, straightforward medium-powered engine, with two cylinders 18 in. diameter by $23\frac{1}{4}$ in. stroke; coupled wheels 5 ft. 1 in. diameter; a total heating surface of 1166 sq. ft. and a grate area of 21.9 sq. ft. The weight of engine only was no more than 45 tons. Though black was the basic livery the use of 'blued' steel for the boiler cladding gave a handsome effect.

135 **Buenos Aires and Rosario Railway:** Two-cylinder Compound 4-6-0 Locomotive.

The railways of the Argentine represent an outstanding example of British business enterprise and development, which was conducted to the great advantage and advancement of the economy and welfare of the country itself. At the turn of the century, and for more than forty years after, the majority of the railways were British-owned, and the equipment was mostly supplied from Great Britain. For many years the two-cylinder compound type of locomotive was very popular, and we illustrate a fine example of the 4-6-0 built in 1904 by the North British Locomotive Company at their Atlas works for the Rosario line, which later became part of the Central Argentine system. It is the high pressure cylinder which is shown in the picture. The diameters were 19 in. high pressure and $27\frac{1}{2}$ in. low pressure, both with a stroke of 26 in. Interesting external features are the solid bogie wheels, the huge headlamp, and the smokebox being unusually large for that period. It included a spark arrester, and a space for deposit of ashes. The Argentine standard gauge is 5 ft. 6 in. and this permitted of a spacious layout between the frames. Other dimensions were the total heating surface of 1634 sq. ft., the grate area of 25 sq. ft. By current standards they were not large engines, having a total weight of 61¼ tons, while the double bogie tender, when fully loaded weighed 40¾ tons.

136 **Buenos Aires Great Southern Railway:** Four-cylinder Compound 4-6-0 Express Locomotive.

This line, affectionately known by all connected with it as the BAGS, was the largest of all the Argentine railways, and was always in the forefront of locomotive development in South America. Like the other Argentine railways it made extensive use of two-cylinder compounds, but just at the end of our period considerable interest was aroused by the construction by the Vulcan Foundry Ltd. of a four-cylinder balanced compound 4-4-2 for the English Great Northern Railway. The locomotive authorities of the BAGS, faced by the ever-increasing weight of express trains, decided to order something similar, but of the 4-6-0 type. The result was the Class 12B four-cylinder compound illustrated. The cylinder proportions were the same as those of the Great Northern 4-4-2 namely 14 in. diameter high pressure, inside and driving on the leading coupled axle, and 23 in. low pressure, outside, driving on the centre coupled axle. The stroke in each case was 26 in. The coupled wheels were 6 ft. 0 in. diameter as on all other BAGS passenger engines. The boiler was a large one, having a total heating surface of 1813 sq. ft. and a grate area of 28 sq. ft. The boiler pressure was 220 lb. per sq. in. Nine engines of this class were built by Vulcan Foundry, and they put in 30 years of express passenger service in the Argentine.

137 **Antofagasta (Chile) and Bolivia Railway:** 0-6-4 Type Tank Engine.

This is one of the lesser-known mountain-climbing railways of the world. It is laid on the 2 ft. 6 in. gauge, and ascends from the port of Antofagasta in the north of Chile to Oruro, in Bolivia. The length of the main line is 574 miles, but in the course of its negotiation of the Andes mountain range it climbs to a height of over 12,000 ft. above sea-level. The gradients in places are very severe, but the traffic is reminiscent of the hey-day of the Festiniog Railway in North Wales, in that the products of the country—minerals, nitrate ores, and such like—are conveyed downhill to the coast, and it is only railway stores that are involved in the long uphill pull inland. At the turn of the century locomotives of a number of interesting types were being suplied from Leeds by the Hunslet Engine Company. The one chosen for illustration is the 0-6-4 tank type, used for shunting and short-distance hauls on the main line. Although the gauge is only 2 ft. 6 in. the loading gauge permits of a locomotive that is very wide in proportion, and the overhang as seen from the front is unusually large. These little tank engines had cylinders 15 in. diameter by 18 in. stroke, coupled wheels 3 ft. 0 in. diameter a total heating surface of 740 sq. ft. with a grate area of 15 sq. ft. Their total weight in working order was 39¼ tons.

138 **Bolivian State Railways:** Fairlie 'Double Engine'.

In Bolivia itself railway conditions are no less severe than on the connecting line to Antofagasta, described in connection with the previous illustration. The rail gauge is also 2 ft. 6 in., and to work on this line the

Fairlie type of locomotive was introduced in 1906. The decision was no doubt influenced by the very successful use of the 'double engine' principle on the Festiniog Railway. The Bolivian engines illustrated were built by the Yorkshire Engine Company, in Leeds and were considerably larger and more powerful than those of the Festiniog Railway. They differed also in having two completely separate boilers. The engines of the latter railway had one double-ended boiler with a firebox in the middle, with the result that the driver stood on one side, and the fireman on the other in places that were confined, and often hot! The Bolivian engines have an orthodox type of cab, but with a firedoor both fore and aft. The two engine units, each of the 0-6-0 type, are on bogies, providing for a very flexible unit. The cylinders were each $12\frac{1}{2}$ in. diameter by 16 in. stroke: the wheels were 2 ft. 6 in. diameter. The total heating surface of the two boilers was 1047 sq. ft. and the total grate area $21\frac{1}{2}$ sq. ft. The tanks had a capacity of 1500 gallons of water, and in neatly arranged coal bunkers, 2 tons of coal. The total weight of the double engine in working order was 52 tons.

139 **Great Northern Railway:** The Ivatt Large-boilered 'Atlantic'.

In connection with Plate 99 the origin of the pioneer British 'Atlantic' the Ivatt No. 990 was described, and in 1902 in furtherance of his policy of providing locomotives of exceptional steaming power he built the first of the large-boilered variety of the same design. Although the steaming capacity was so greatly increased the cylinder dimensions remained unchanged. It is no exaggeration to say that the new engines created perhaps a greater impression than any other contemporary design, and the girth of the boiler was seized upon by the railway advertising men of the day to accentuate the potentialities of Great Northern engines. Actually, while it could not be said that the performance of the new engines was disappointing, they did not come fully into their own until many years later, after Sir Nigel Gresley had succeeded Ivatt as Locomotive Superintendent of the Great Northern Railway. Then, high-degree superheating was applied to them, and they became remarkable engines, capable of deputizing for a 'Pacific' on the heaviest Anglo-Scottish express duties. Our illustration shows one of the engines as originally built. The subsequent external changes were so slight as to pass almost unnoticed except to an experienced connoisseur of locomotive practice.

140 **Palatinate Railway, Germany:** 'Atlantic' type Express Locomotive.

This book includes many examples of 'Atlantic' type engines, a wheel arrangement that originated in the U.S.A. Its first introduction in England and on the continent of Europe took place in the same year, 1898. The English example was the Great Northern 'Klondyke' (Plate 99), and the Palatinate illustrated here was the first on the Continent. It was built by Krauss & Co. of Munich for the international express trains following the Valley of the Rhine from Rotterdam to Basle, but confined of course to the Palatinate section between Bingerbruck and Weissenburg. They had a specified performance of 62 m.p.h. on the level with a load of 220 tons. Dimensionally these locomotives are not so powerful as they might appear, with cylinders $19\frac{5}{16}$ in. diameter by $22\frac{7}{16}$ in. stroke, and coupled wheels 6 ft. 6 in. The boiler was large, with a total heating surface of 2060 sq. ft. and the grate area large also, for satisfactory burning of soft German coal, $30\frac{1}{4}$ sq. ft. An interesting feature is the double framing in the region of the coupled wheels, and the conical-fronted smokebox and wedge-shaped front of the cab were doubtless designed to lessen air resistance, though this would not be very great at the maximum speed of 62 m.p.h. then permitted on these German express routes.

141 **Prussian State Railway:** A Superheater 4-4-0 Express Locomotive.

British locomotive practice over the years came to incorporate as standard features several outstanding devices developed overseas, and among these there is no more remarkable example than the superheater, brought to a high degree of efficiency by Dr Wilhelm Schmidt of Berlin. The Prussian locomotive illustrated is one of the earliest examples fitted with the Schmidt superheater and including the inventor's own design of piston valves, actuated by the Walschaerts valve gear, the latter a Belgian invention. The Prussian engine was a large and powerful machine for its day, with two cylinders $20\frac{3}{4}$ in. diameter by $23\frac{1}{2}$ in. stroke, and coupled wheels 6 ft. 7 in. diameter. With superheated steam a somewhat smaller boiler and lower steam pressure can be satisfactorily used, and the engine had a total heating surface of 1440 sq. ft, grate area of 24.3 sq. ft, and worked at a pressure of 170 lb. per sq. in. The Schmidt superheater was subsequently adopted as a standard on the London and North Western Railway, and in 1910 when the first superheater engine was under construction at Crewe Dr Schmidt travelled to England and personally supervised the setting of the valves.

142 **State Railway of Saxony:** A Two-cylinder compound 4-4-0.

In contrast to the smartness and efficiency of railways in north Germany, the railways in the southern states at the turn of the century displayed an easy going and leisurely attitude towards the working of traffic, and those passengers who travelled through from Paris to the Balkans by the far-famed Orient Express could not fail to notice how slow the progress was through south Germany. Nevertheless some fine and technically interesting locomotives were to be seen at work, and the practice of the Munich firm of Maffei provided inspiration for several famous locomotive developments. The engine illustrated is one of the popular two-cylinder compound type, of which there were both German (Von Borries) and Austrian (Gölsdorf) varieties. With outside cylinders the appearance from the front was somewhat odd, because from that standpoint one could see that the cylinders were of different sizes. On this Saxon engine the high pressure cylinder was $18\frac{1}{2}$ in. diameter and the low pressure no less than $27\frac{1}{4}$ in. Both had stroke of 24 in. The firebox, with a grate area of 20 sq. ft., was of the Belpaire type (a Belgian invention); the coupled wheels were 5 ft. 3 in. diameter, and the boiler pressure 185 lb. per sq. in.

143 **Egyptian State Railways:** 2-2-2 Express Passenger Locomotive.

At the period of this book the locomotive department of this railway was under the superintendency of Mr F. H. Trevithick, one of the grandsons of the great Cornish pioneer. He took over a somewhat heterogeneous collection of locomotives, but by skilful rebuilding at the works situated at Boulac, Cairo, he produced some excellent machines. One of these rebuildings was that of some Stephenson-built 2-2-2s, which had a stove pipe chimney, a rather odd-looking dome, and a large canopied cab, which latter with a large amount of side sheeting, could be very hot. Mr Trevithick's rebuild of these engines of 1868 produced a beautiful little 2-2-2 similar to that illustrated, and turned out of Boulac shops in 1893. Apart from their open, awning-like cabs they might have been Great Western express engines of the Armstrong–Dean era, operating on the narrow gauge sections of the line. This rebuilding produced two engines additional to the new 2-2-2s delivered from England in 1889, illustrated in our picture, and which were somewhat larger than the rebuilds. The crimson-lake livery was introduced with these engines of 1889 and remained an Egyptian standard for many years. The new engines of 1889 had cylinders $17\frac{1}{2}$ in. diameter by 24 in. stroke, and 7 ft. driving wheels. There were six of the 1889 series built by Kitsons' of Leeds, to which four more were subsequently purchased from the Franco-Belge Company at La Coyère in 1894. With these ten new engines and the two rebuilds the Egyptian State Railways had a most efficient stud of engines for working the Cairo–Alexandria expresses.

144 **Egyptian State Railways:** 2-4-0 Light Tank Engine, on Extended Loan.

This pretty little engine has been chosen for inclusion because it illustrates how the standard products of British manufacturers found their way into unexpected quarters. If one discards the oriental cab and spark-arresting chimney the familiar 2-4-0 side tank engine of Beyer–Peacock design used on the Isle of Man railways and elsewhere is revealed. These Egyptian engines were, however, not built for the Government railway but for the Diara Sanieh Sugar Estates. They came to work on the Egyptian State Railways in these unusual circumstances. In 1897 the Embabeh bridge over the Nile at Cairo began to show signs of structural defects, and for a time it was completely closed to railway traffic. Trains for Upper Egypt had to start from Boulac Dacrour station on the west bank, and the express engines had to be stabled in the open. Then after temporary repairs had been made to the bridge authority was given for the express engines to cross, but only as light engines. The trains themselves had to be drawn by a light locomotive. The Government accordingly borrowed a number of these little 2-4-0 tanks from the Sugar Estates Railway, and they were used for some considerable time. They had cylinders 12 in. diameter by 18 in. stroke, and coupled wheels 4 ft. 1 in. diameter. The fuel used was sugar-cane refuse; hence the spark-arresting chimneys!

145 **Egyptian State Railways:** 'Atlantic' Type Express Locomotive.

In describing certain large Indian locomotives, and particularly under reference 117, the practice was referred to of having locomotives of otherwise identical design, but arranged variously as 'Atlantics' or 4-6-0s. Certain experiments in Egypt actually preceded the similar trials in India, and on the English Great Central and Great Western Railways. In 1900 the engine illustrated in our picture was purchased from the Brooks Locomotive Works, Dunkirk, New York, and it was so designed as to be convertible at will from a 4-4-2 to a 4-6-0. Unlike the English and Indian types, as a 4-4-2 this Egyptian engine had 6 ft. 6 in. coupled wheels, whereas when running as a 4-6-0 it had 5 ft. 0 in. coupled wheels. This Egyptian experiment was thus not a straight comparison between the 4-4-2 and 4-6-0 types for the same duty, as in England and India, but rather the use of the same chassis, boiler and cylinders for an Atlantic express engine, on the one hand, and a 4-6-0 mixed traffic engine on the other. The cylinders were 20 in. diameter by 26 in. stroke; the boiler had a total heating surface of 2008 sq. ft. and the working pressure was 180 lb. sq. in. The design actually permitted of a third variation, namely that of a 4-6-0 with 5 ft. 9 in. coupled wheels.

146 **Egyptian State Railway:** 4-4-0 Express Passenger Locomotive.

One of the great problems in operating railways in a country like Egypt is that of water supply, and in the early 1900s the Locomotive Superintendent, F. H. Trevithick, made a long series of experiments with various forms of feed-water heaters to try and effect a reduction in water consumption. Our picture illustrates one of the handsome 4-4-0 express passenger engines built by Neilson Reid & Co. in 1902. This was the standard type on the Cairo–Alexandria expresses for many years, but the one illustrated is fitted with the Worthington feed-water heater, which can be seen just ahead of the cab on the right-hand side. The equipment also included a tubular heater for the exhaust gases. As originally built these engines were a typically simple and straight-forward British product of the day, with cylinders 18 in. diameter by 24 in. stroke; 6 ft. 3 in. diameter coupled wheels; a relatively small boiler providing a total of 1235 sq. ft. heating surface, and carried a pressure of 160 lb. per sq. in. They were fast and successful engines, and Trevithick's experiments with them led eventually to the adoption of superheating. This, as on all other railways, gave great economies in coal and water consumption with the simplest of apparatus.

147 **Italian Southern Railway:** Four-cylinder Compound 0-6-4 Locomotive.

Of all the systems of compounding used on the railways of the world none was more original or, in retrospect, more curious than that devised by Signor Planchard, the director of motive power on the Italian Southern Railway. First of all, to provide the engine-men with a good look-out, he turned the engine back-to-front, as it were. While there was no difficulty in having the water supply on a tender trailing behind the smokebox end of the engine, the coal had to be carried in bunkers on either side of the firebox, and each of these bunkers had a capacity of 2 tons. The engines were four-cylinder compounds, and to make everything accessible all four cylinders were arranged ahead of the smokebox. But instead of having the 'engine' truly divided as in other four-cylinder compound systems Signot Planchard put both high pressure cylinders on one side and both low pressure on the other—thus perpetuating the inequality in weight of moving parts inherent in the Wordell–Von Borries and Gölsdorf systems of compounding. By these means he simplified the cross connections between cylinders, but the inside cylinders, one high pressure and one low pressure, had to be arranged with their centre lines steeply inclined, to drive, like the outside cylinders, on to the centre pair of coupled wheels. These engines were designed for fast running, having 6 ft. $3\frac{1}{2}$ in. coupled wheels, a boiler with a total heating surface of 1650 sq. ft., grate area of 32 sq. ft., and working at a pressure of 213 lb. per sq. in. The cylinder diameters were $14\frac{1}{8}$ in. high pressure and $23\frac{1}{8}$ low pressure, with a common stroke of $25\frac{1}{2}$ in.

148 **Italian Mediterranean Railway:** Two-cylinder Compound 4-6-0.

In contrast to the Southern Railway the Mediterranean line for its express services on the coastal route between Rome and Pisa used compound 4-6-0s, of more orthodox layout, but with only two cylinders. Like Signor Planchard's 'back-to-front' 0-6-4s which were built by Borsig's of Berlin, the Mediterranean engines were also built in Germany, but by Maffei of Munich. The contract stipulated a sustained maximum speed of 58 m.p.h. on the level, with an average load of 220 tons. This would have been considered a very modest requirement on an English railway even in the 1900–5 period, where speeds of over 70 m.p.h. with 300-ton trains were then becoming quite commonplace. The two cylinders of the Italian 4-6-0 had diameters of $21\frac{3}{4}$ in. high pressure and 31 in. low pressure, with a common stroke of $26\frac{3}{4}$ in. The coupled wheels were 6 ft. diameter, the total heating surface only 1413 sq. ft.; the grate area 28 sq. ft., and the working pressure 185 lb. per sq. in. The tenders were unusually small, having a capacity of only 2860 gallons of water and 3 tons of coal. A cross-reference may be made here to the tenders of 'Dunalastair' 4-4-0s adopted as standard by the Belgian railways which had a tender tank capacity of no less than 4125 gallons.

149 **Italian Mediterranean Railway:** Compound 4-8-0 Mixed Traffic Engine.

While the main line from Genoa to Rome, following the coast for much of the way, has relatively easy gradients this railway has always been a major operating problem on the very severe Ronco incline through which the main line from Turin to Genoa cuts through the Ligurian Alps in a precipitous descent of 1 in 60 to the coastal plain. These 4-8-0s were introduced in 1903 to work freight trains of 500 tons up the incline at a speed of not less than $12\frac{1}{2}$ m.p.h. Although designed primarily for freight their great tractive power was also utilized for working passenger trains on the Ronco incline without double heading or rear-end banking, and they successfully handled loads of 150 to 200 tons at speeds of about 25 m.p.h. These very successful engines, of which thirty were built in 1903 by the Societa Italiana Ernesto Breda of Milan, had cylinders $21\frac{1}{4}$ in. high pressure and $31\frac{1}{2}$ in. low pressure, with a common stroke of $26\frac{3}{4}$ in. Coupled wheels were 4 ft. 7 in. diameter. The boiler was not so big as might be expected for such heavy duty, having a total heating surface of 1719 sq. ft. This railway, however, used best quality Welsh coal, shipped in a fleet of colliers of their own, which used to ply between Genoa and Cardiff.

150 **Western Railway of France:** de Glehn Compound 4-6-0.

While the Northern and the Orléans railways in France used the 'Atlantic' type of locomotive for their fastest trains the Western and the Eastern preferred the 4-6-0. There was, in France, the same diversity of preference in wheel arrangement as was to be seen in England at the same time. In France, however, there was no direct trials on the same railway with comparable designs having alternatively the 4-4-2 and 4-6-0 wheel arrangements, as on the English Great Central, Great Western, and the North Eastern railways. The Western Railway of France certainly had some heavily graded routes in Brittany and on the English boat train route from Dieppe over that part of line between Dieppe and Rouen. Even so, it was not until the summer of 1903 that these trains were accelerated to a run of 160 minutes over the $125\frac{1}{2}$ miles between Paris and Dieppe. Previously to that the time had been the level three hours, which was, of course, a much more leisurely schedule than that of the Nord expresses between Paris and Calais which averaged nearly 55 m.p.h. Although they were not called upon for very heavy work, the Western compound 4-6-0s were excellent engines, and did their work most economically.

151 **Cape Government Railways:** 4-6-0 Passenger and Goods Locomotive.

This illustration shows a type of locomotive that was at one time becoming a standard design throughout South Africa. They were used not only on the lines within the colony of the Cape of Good Hope. They were also used in the Orange Free State and on the Rhodesia Railways, between Mafeking and Bulawayo. A number of these engines had six-wheeled tenders for coal burning, but the one illustrated is oil-burning, with a much larger tender. Although very British in style the design was worked out in South Africa, and include a number of interesting detail features. The distinctive style of bogie wheel will be noted, also the single slide bar, with the cross-head slung from it. The headlight is one of the old type, oil lit. These engines were in very widespread use at the turn of the century, working passenger and goods trains alike. They worked the bulk of the military traffic from the Cape. The cylinders were 17 in. diameter by 26 in. stroke; coupled wheel diameter 4 ft. 6 in., and the special design of bogie wheels 2 ft. $4\frac{1}{2}$ in. diameter. The boiler was not large compared with some of the post-war Transvaal engines, having a total heating surface of only 1122 sq. ft. and a grate area of 18 sq. ft. Nevertheless, as South African 'maids of all work', they rank as a notable design.

152 **Cape Government Railway:** American-built 'Atlantic' Locomotive.

In 1898 the locomotive 'famine' which affected so many European countries also hit South Africa, and the Baldwin Locomotive Company supplied Atlantic engines to the Cape Government Railways. At that time the Atlantic type itself was still something of a novelty, and this American-built South African engine was delivered at almost exactly the same time as the first British Atlantic took the road (see reference 99). The Cape engine, running on the 3 ft. 6 in. gauge, was a much smaller version than the Great Northern 'Klondyke,' and had cylinders 16 in. diameter by 22 in. stroke the coupled wheels were 4 ft. 8 in. diameter, and the boiler was of typical American proportions with a total heating surface of 1560 sq. ft. and a grate area of 30 sq. ft. Externally, it was a characteristic Baldwin job of that period, with a very large cab; bar-frames for the tender bogies, and inside valve gear. The finish, with polished brass bands on the boiler, and some fanciful lining on the cab and tender, was quite ornate, and savoured of the garishly adorned American locomotives of the nineteenth century. By comparison with contemporary British locomotives it was a diminutive little thing, weighing only $45\frac{1}{4}$ tons, and 73 tons with its tender.

153 **Natal Government Railways:** 4-10-2 Main Line Passenger Tank Engine.

At the period covered by this book there must have been very few ten-coupled engines to be found anywhere in the world. The type illustrated was designed by Mr G. Reid, Locomotive Superintendent at Durban, for working over the very steep gradients leading from the coast of Natal to the central plateau. They were built by Dübs & Co. in Glasgow, and assembled in Durban. Ten of these engines were supplied and they arrived during the closing stages of the South African War. At the end of the year 1901 they were purchased by the Imperial Government for use in the Transvaal where the railways and rolling-stock had been badly affected by the war. As thus reallocated they were stationed at Volksrust and Pretoria and took a share in the working of every class of traffic except the mail trains. They had cylinders 19 in. diameter by 27 in. stroke; coupled wheels 3 ft. 9 in. diameter, and carried a boiler pressure of 160 lb. per sq. in. The total weight in working order was $68\frac{1}{2}$ tons. Our picture shows one of these engines in the colours of the Natal Government Railways. When reallocated to the Central South African Railway (Transvaal) they were painted black, with red and white dividing lines, but retained their polished brass domes. The engines did so well on their new duties that a further order was placed for additional engines of the class, and deliveries were made in 1903.

154 **Natal Government Railways:** 4-8-2 Standard Tank Engine.

This was the standard type of locomotive used in Natal until the arrival of the large 4-10-2s (ref. 153). After the transfer of the latter engines the 4-8-2s were left virtually in sole possession. In 1901 there were over 120 of them at work, and except for a few older classes engaged in shunting no other type of engine was in use. They worked the mail trains between Durban and Pretoria, all the intermediate classes of trains conveying passengers, and all the goods. For those who yearn for extreme standardization of motive power the Natal Government Railways of nearly seventy years must have seemed something very near to Utopia! Like the large 4-10-2 engines these 4-8-2s were built by Dübs & Co. The coupled wheels were only 3 ft. in diameter. This, while making the engines very reliable in climbing the heavy gradients precluded any fast running. Actually there was little difference in the running speeds of passenger and goods trains. All the rolling-stock was fitted with the automatic vacuum brake, which meant that heavy loads could be adequately controlled on the steep descending gradients. The cylinders were 17 in. diameter by 21 in. stroke, and the slide valves actuated by Stephenson's link motion. The boiler had a total heating surface of 1076 sq. ft. and the grate area was 15.7 sq. ft. The total weight of the engine in working order was 45 tons.

155 **Great Central Railway:** Pollitt 4-2-2 Express Locomotive for the London Extension.

The audacious move of the Manchester, Sheffield and Lincolnshire Railway in projecting an extension southwards from the Nottinghamshire colliery area, which had hitherto formed its most southernly extent was bitterly opposed by all existing railways; but the Bill received Parliamentary sanction, and the line was built to link up with the Metropolitan Railway at Quainton Road Junction, near Aylesbury, and a service of fast express trains planned, in strong competition with all other north-going lines from London. The name was changed to the Great Central, and to attract traffic speeds had to be high. For the new trains a series of fine 4-2-2 'singles' was built, one of which is shown in our picture. They had the stove-pipe chimneys that had been characteristic of the Manchester, Sheffield and Lincolnshire Railway for some years, and had a generally distinctive appearance necessary to attract attention to the new service. They were very powerful engines for the 4-2-2 type, having cylinders $19\frac{1}{2}$ in. diameter by 26 in. stroke driving wheels were 7 ft. 9 in. diameter, and the boiler was of the standard type used by Mr Pollitt's 4-4-0 and 0-6-0 engines, with Belpaire firebox. With the light trains on the London extension these new 4-2-2s did good work between Marylebone and Leicester. Coupled engines were used on the more heavily graded sections north of Leicester.

156 **Bombay, Baroda and Central India Railway:** American-built 4-4-0 Express Locomotive.

The Bombay, Baroda and Central India Railway runs northwards from Bombay and like the Indian railway generally had a strong British flavour; most of the rolling-stock and fixed equipment was British built, and the senior staff were all British. At the turn of the century, however, when increasing traffic in most parts of the world caused a general shortage of locomotives, the only way in which delivery of new locomotives could be obtained quickly was by purchasing from the U.S.A. and the Bombay, Baroda and Central India Railway obtained some interesting 4-4-0 express passenger engines from Baldwins in 1902. At first sight they appear as un-English as one could imagine; but if one could imagine the running-plate lowered to the normal British position, just above the upper slide bar, and splashers provided for the coupled wheels, one has a very pretty and conventional locomotive. This is a remarkable example of what the height of the running-plate can do to the appearance of a locomotive. The cylinders were 18 in. diameter by 26 in. stroke, the coupled wheels were 6 ft. 2 in. diameter, and the boiler provided $1281\frac{1}{2}$ sq. ft. of heating surface and a grate area of $22\frac{1}{2}$ sq. ft. The boiler pressure was 160 lb. sq. in.

157 **Waterford, Limerick and Western Railway:** 0-6-0 Goods Engine.

This railway ran from east to west across the southern part of Ireland, intersecting the main line of the Great Southern and Western at Limerick Junction. Its separate existence came to an end on 31 December 1900, when it was absorbed by the Great Southern and Western Railways. The locomotive stock of the Waterford line, in its independent days, is of interest to students of locomotive development because the engineer was J. G. Robinson, who afterwards went to the Great Central to succeed Harry Pollitt. The 0-6-0 goods engine in our picture was Robinson's last design for the Waterford, Limerick, and Western Railway just as the 4-2-2 express engine on the facing page was Pollitt's last for the Great Central. The Waterford, Limerick, and Western Railway goods engine is typical of the very handsome lines Robinson contrived to design into all his engines, and it was not long before his elegantly styled chimneys, as evident on the Irish goods engine, were appearing on Great Central engines in place of the old 'stove-pipes' of Parker and

Pollitt. The Waterford, Limerick, and Western Railway 0-6-0s had cylinders 17 in. diameter by 24 in. stroke; coupled wheels were 5 ft. 2 in. diameter, and the boiler had a total heating surface of 981 sq. ft. They were, of course, no more than medium-powered engines, and the boiler pressure was only 150 lb. per sq. in. But as example of neatness and symmetry in design they would be hard to beat.

158 **Atchison, Topeka & Santa Fé Railway:** 4-6-0 Tandem Compound Express Engine.

The Santa Fé in recent years has provided some of the finest steam locomotive work to be witnessed anywhere in the world, with the giant 4-8-4 oil-fired locomotives working through between Chicago and Los Angeles on very fast and heavy trains. At the turn of the century Mr John Player was Superintendent of Machinery, and in 1900 he introduced the interesting 4-6-0 locomotive illustrated. Engines of generally similar proportions, but arranged as two-cylinder simples, were in regular use, but in turning to compounds Mr Player used the 'tandem' arrangement in which the axis of the high and low pressure cylinders on each side of the locomotive was coincident and both drove the same piston rod. The high pressure cylinders were forward, with a diameter of 14 in., and the low pressure were aft, with a diameter of 24 in. The stroke was 28 in., as in the simple 4-6-0s of a slightly earlier vintage. The simple engines had cylinders 19½ in. diameter. On the compounds the coupled wheel diameter was 6 ft. 5 in., the boiler had a total heating surface of 1915 sq. ft., and a grate area of 26½ sq. ft. These were large and heavy engines weighing 75 tons without their tenders.

159 **New Zealand Government Railway:** 'Turtle-back' Bogie Passenger Carriage of 1903.

This was a period of rapid expansion of railway business in New Zealand, and carriage design having remained traditional with the 'bird-cage' type (ref. 92) began to develop quickly. The bird-cage vestibule extending only half way was abandoned and the corridor was extended throughout the length of the vehicle, but still open! It gave access to a series of compartments and the lavatory was in the middle. The coaches of the 1899–90 period had clerestory roofs and were used on the South Island main line express trains. They were followed by the turtle-back cars. In Great Britain they would have been styled 'elliptical-roofed'. As our picture shows they were a neat design, and it was a form that was to be familiar to passengers in New Zealand for more than fifty years. They were lightly constructed, and had a tare weight of only 13 to 14 tons. Platform gates and hand-rails to facilitate passage between the cars were added in 1910. A characteristic of New Zealand carriages was the very short wheelbase bogie. At the time of their construction gas lighting was standard. It is remarkable also to recall that it was only in the year 1901 that the New Zealand railways decided to equip all stock with continuous automatic brakes. They chose the Westinghouse. Until that time main line coaching stock had hand-brakes only.

160 **New Zealand Government Railway:** 'Wf' Class 2-6-4 Tank Engine.

In 1908 the Government incorporated the Wellington and Manawatu Railway into the national system, the project that the original promoters had in mind came at last to fruition. This was the completion of the trunk line of communication in the North Island between Auckland and Wellington. In linking up the hitherto isolated extremities the line passed through a high mountainous region, within sight of some active volcanoes, and a journey from end to end was something of an adventure. The 'Wf' 2-6-4 tank engine No. 386, the subject of our picture, was used on part of the journey of the first through train, in August 1908. Fifty years later the Golden Jubilee of the line was celebrated with great enthusiasm, and as the veteran tank engine was still in existence arrangements were made for her to be included. Near to point where the last spike had been driven in in 1908 by the then Prime Minister of New Zealand is the railway town of Taumarunui and the Mayor of this town purchased old 386 from the Railways Department of the New Zealand Government and presented it to the town during the Golden Jubilee celebrations. The engine is now enthroned in front of the station as an historical relic.

161 **New Zealand Government Railways:** 4-6-0 Express Passenger Locomotive of 1898.

While in the North Island the Wellington and Manawatu Railway was beginning to use 4-6-0s, the Government railway in the South Island has already established the 4-6-0 type with the 'UA' class from England, and the very popular 'UB' class now illustrated in our picture. They worked on the Christchurch–Dunedin express service, taking these important trains as far south as Timarsu. The 'UB' class came from the Baldwin Locomotive Company and were very similar in appearance to the Manawatu engines. Curiously enough, while the 'UB' engines were very popular with their crews, certain outside observers sought to criticize them severely—one point being emphasized was that the firebox extended so far backwards into the cab as to make impossible communication between the driver and fireman, in their accustomed position one on either side of the firebox. A further batch of ten engines was supplied by Baldwin's in 1901, which differed from the engine illustrated in having the Walschaerts valve gear and piston valves, instead of slide valves actuated by Stephenson link motion on the first ten. Both varieties had cylinders 16 in. diameter by 20 in. stroke, coupled wheels 4 ft. 1 in. diameter, a total heating surface of 1324 sq. ft., and a grate area of 16 sq. ft. The boiler pressure was 200 lb. per sq. in.

162 **New Zealand Government Railway:** Class 'UC' 4-6-0 Passenger Engine of 1901.

Although the railway administration had placed some reliance on the import of locomotives from the U.S.A. the Addington Works in 1892 prepared an original design for a 4-6-0, and several examples were built in New Zealand between 1894 and 1899. Prior to this latter date, however, traffic was increasing to such an extent in the South Island that authority was given for the purchase of six more 4-6-0 locomotives. The Class 'U' engines designed at Addington had a distinctly British appearance, and the contract for the new engines was awarded to Sharp Stewart & Co. of Glasgow, one of the constituent firms of the North British Locomotive Co. Ltd. These engines were very popular in New Zealand, and in 1901 ten more slightly larger engines of the same general design were also supplied from Glasgow. These were the 'UC' class, and had the following dimensions: cylinders 16 in. diameter by 22 in. stroke; coupled wheels 4 ft. 1 in. diameter; total heating surface 975 sq. ft.; grate area 17 sq. ft.; boiler pressure 200 lb. per sq. in. The 1901 series, shown in our picture, were distinguished from the earlier ones by having piston valves and a running-plate raised above the coupled wheels. Of British manufacture they had plate frames in contrast to their American contemporaries in New Zealand.

163 **Central South African Railway:** Main Line Bogie Carriage.

Following the end of the war, in 1901, intense efforts were made to develop railway communications in South Africa, and for the through expresses between the Cape and the cities of the Transvaal some extremely fine new trains were put into service. Our picture illustrates a first-class saloon having an observation lounge and a saloon portion which can be adapted either for day or night travel. It formed part of a six-car luxury train, of which the make-up was as follows: (*a*) day saloon/sleeping; baggage car (*b*) day saloon and sleeping car (*c*) dining car (*d*) day saloon and sleeping car (*e*) day saloon and sleeping car (*f*) the car illustrated, which provided the observation lounge on the rear end of the train. The whole train was equipped in the most luxurious style, and although running on the South African standard 3 ft. 6 in. gauge the coaches were as wide as the normal British vehicles of the latest and widest type running at that period. Each of the six cars was 60 ft. 3 in. over the body, with a width of 9 ft. 1 in. At a time when gas lighting was general, even on the crack expresses of Great Britain, this train was electrically lighted throughout. The interiors were beautifully furnished, in a quiet type of upholstery and decoration. The trains were constructed by the Metropolitan Amalgamated Railway Carriage and Wagon Company of Birmingham.

164 **Belgian State Railways:** Second-class Bogie Vestibuled Carriage.

In the latter part of the nineteenth century the Belgian State Railways were among the most backward in Europe, in respect of the quaintness and antiquity of locomotives and rolling-stock. Then, however, there came a great revival; the five 'Dunalastair' 4-4-0 locomotives (ref. 17) imported from Scotland set new standards in engine design and construction, and this followed by the introduction of some fine new bogie coaches for the through express trains running between Brussels and the major cities and ports. The second-class carriage illustrated is typical of the stock on these new trains. The seating was spacious and luxurious with only three aside in the seven compartments. As usual with Continental stock doors were provided at the ends, but in view of the general lavishness of the accommodation it is surprising to find that these corridor coaches included no lavatories. As usual, the exterior was very plain. Nevertheless a train of these handsomely proportioned coaches, however plain in their exteriors, looked very fine running behind a 'Dunalastair' type 4-4-0 locomotive, whether the latter was in the original Scottish blue (ref. 17) or in the standard Belgian brown (ref. 169).

165 **Moscow–Brest Railway:** Restaurant Car.

In several of the illustrations in this book reference has been made to the extraordinary differences that existed at the end of the nineteenth century in standards of carriage comfort, and of decoration—both interior and exterior. One can perhaps understand that no adornments were lavished upon fourth-class carriages for semi-express trains, or that trains like the Cote d'Azur Pullman and the Interstate express running between Melbourne and Adelaide should be the height of luxury. But the subject of our present picture, the restaurant cars working, in 1900, on the principal express trains between Moscow and Warsaw are somewhat perplexing. The exterior in its plainness is characteristic of most European carriages of the period; but internally quite a lot of space was given up to the kitchen, and accommodation for the staff, while the central portion formed an open saloon with seats for only twenty-four passengers. Plenty of attention was given to the provision of heating, but it was evidently intended to convey the romantic aura of a dimly-lit beer cellar for those taking meals, because in the saloon the windows were meagre, and the only lighting came from four small candle lamps.

166 **Midland Railway:** Pullman-type Sleeping Carriage.

It might perhaps be considered that one is carrying comparisons to an unfair extent in setting one of these extremely elegant and superbly finished vehicles immediately beside some of their Continental contemporaries. It does exemplify the great difference that then existed between British styles of finish and those prevalent elsewhere. These beautiful coaches built for the Midland, Scottish night express services had Pullman-type bodies and standard Midland bogies. They provided sleeping accommodation for eleven passengers only, five in traversely arranged beds, in what were termed 'separate state rooms'—like the present-day first-class sleepers on British Railways—and six longitudinal bunks in an open saloon, each curtained off from view from the rest. This latter arrangement followed the style of contemporary American sleepers. The use of these Pullman-type cars on the Anglo-Scottish services led, on the Glasgow and South Western Railway, to all expresses running through from Glasgow to English destinations being known generally as 'Pullmans', whether they included a Pullman-type car or not. The nickname, indeed, survived long after the Pullman cars had been replaced by vehicles of wholly British design.

167 **Dutch Rhenish Railway:** 4-4-0 Express Passenger Locomotive, 'Rhine Bogie'.

This was one of the earliest railways in the Netherlands having its first section, between Amsterdam and Utrecht, opened in 1843. It had actually been promoted five years earlier but the Dutch Parliament had thrown out the Bill. The King thereupon stepped in and by royal command ordered the building of the line! It was very much a child of British enterprise, however, and when the company was formed to work it no less than 67 per cent of the shares were held by British people. It eventually extended to Arnhem and then to the German frontier at Emmerich. The influence remained strongly British until 1890, when the major part of the line was absorbed into the Dutch State Railway. Just prior to that, in 1889, the Rhenish Company had introduced the first of the celebrated 'Rhine Bogie' 4-4-0s from Sharp Stewart's Atlas Works, Glasgow. These splendid engines immediately proved very popular, and after the partition of the Rhenish system between the State and the Holland Railway the latter took over all the original nine 'Rhine Bogies', and subsequently ordered many more, up to 1903, until the total was forty-seven. The cylinders were 18 in. diameter by 26 in. stroke; coupled wheel diameter was 6 ft. 7 in. A beautiful example of one of these engines, restored to its original livery as shown in our picture, is preserved in the railway museum at Utrecht.

168 **North Brabant German Railway:** 4-6-0 Express Passenger Locomotive.

In the years before the First World War there was great competition for the Anglo-German mail traffic via Flushing. The Dutch State Railway had the principal route, which reached the German frontier at Venlo, but in 1873 a company with international connections was formed to work from Boxtel on the State railway to Wesel on the Rhine, by the exercise of perpetual running powers over a section of the Prussian State Railway between Büderich and Wesel. Competition was very severe and very little traffic passed over the line until it secured the Flushing mail business from 1881 onwards. The North Brabant remained a very small concern, though an important link in the Anglo-German traffic until 1914. Then, of course, the German part of the line was taken over, and the remainder passed into the Dutch State system as from 1919. The mail trains were heavy, often loading to over 400 tons, and in 1908 the company purchased six magnificent 4-6-0 engines from Beyer, Peacock & Co. They were very English in appearance, as shown in our picture, and so far as boiler mountings were concerned had a strong flavour of the Great Central Railway. Their finish was gorgeous, as can be appreciated from the fine model of one of them displayed in the Railway museum at Utrecht. The cylinders were 19 in. diameter by 26 in. stroke; coupled wheels 6 ft. diameter. On the Brabant line of the speed was limited to a maximum of 56 m.p.h. but in later years they were permitted to run up to a maximum of 68 m.p.h.

169 **Belgian State Railways:** Belgian-built 'Dunalastair' type 4-4-0 Locomotive.

Under reference 17 in this book there is described and illustrated one of the five celebrated 'Dunalastair II' class engines of the Caledonian Railway purchased, in all their native Scottish finery, by the Belgian Government in 1898. The type was a great success in Belgium, so much so that with very little modification it was adopted as a national standard and many more of the type were built by Belgian firms. So far as can be traced, however, the famous Caledonian livery was confined only to those imported from Scotland, and the subject of our present picture, one of a batch built in 1903 by the Société Anonyme de St Leonard of Liege, is shown in the style standard on the State Railway at that time, and depicted on a fine model of one of these engines displayed in the Belgian railway museum at Brussels' Nord station. The Scottish-built engines differed from those of the Caledonian proper in having right-hand drive, and the Belgian-built engines had further detail changes, notably in the form of safety valve, the side-windowed cab, and the rather ugly *capuchon*, or lip to the chimney. The Scottish-built engines had an even uglier lip added to their chimneys. The finish, as will be seen from our picture, was very plain, in a livery best described as 'gravy brown'.

170 **Belgian State Railways:** Four-cylinder 4-6-0 Express Locomotives.

From the introduction of the 'Dunalastair' 4-4-0s as a standard type, the Belgian State Railways began to move forward to much larger and more powerful locomotives. In 1905 two new engines were built for trial purposes—one a four-cylinder compound, and the other a four-cylinder simple. As a result of trials of these two engines the simple system was chosen as a future standard. They were strikingly handsome machines, clearly indicating the British influence that had resulted from the introduction of the Scottish-built 'Dunalastairs'. In this respect the Belgian authorities seemed to have turned their backs completely on the quaint practices that had prevailed practically throughout the nineteenth century, including such extraordinary features as *square* funnels. The new 4-6-0s introduced a new style of painting in Belgium, in the subdued olive green, with almost invisible lining out. It is interesting to recall that in a period somewhat later than that of this book the Netherlands State Railways not only adopted the same shade of olive green as their standard locomotive livery, but also introduced a four-cylinder 4-6-0 locomotive design that bore some points of resemblance to the Belgian engines of 1905.

171 **Caledonian Railway:** 30-ton Mineral Wagon.

A feature of British railway freight working that has always been the subject of much comment and adverse criticism is the preponderance of small four-wheeled wagons, whether for conveyance of minerals, or consignments requiring covered vans, or even special traffics such as meat or fish. Furthermore, the typical British goods wagon is of relatively short wheelbase, making it unsuitable for haulage in trains greatly exceeding 50 m.p.h. It is not for want of trying that railway administrations have failed to 'escape' from the short-wheelbase four-wheeled incubus; but larger vehicles have in the past been difficult to accommodate in the sidings of private firms, and particularly in collieries. The Caledonian 30-tonner that we illustrate is a fine example of a high capacity wagon, built in 1903, and it was intended that these vehicles would be run in set trains, rather than incorporated indiscriminately in mixed goods trains. They were fitted with the Westinghouse automatic air brake, as standard on the Caledonian Railway, to permit of safe handling of very heavy loads on steep gradients. One has to record, however, that as on other British railways the large bogie mineral wagons never came into general use for the carrying of coal.

172 **East Indian Railway:** Mineral Oil Tank Wagon.

This was a very interesting design of wagon of which a number were built in 1896 for the East Indian Railway by the Leeds Forge Company. Inside the outer sheeting, which was of galvanized iron, there was a cylindrical tank 22 ft. long and 5 ft. 4 in. diameter outside. It was unusual for that early period in being entirely welded. The tank was divided internally into three sections, but with large apertures at the bottom to enable the oil to flow freely from one section to another. Filling was from the top, and the ladder shown in our picture provides access to one of the filling caps. It is interesting to recall that these wagons were designed to work in conjunction with a scheme of mechanized delivery of the oil at the destination point. The hand wheels at the end were for controlling two rotary pumps for forcing the oil into the elevated tanks at the depots. Each pump was capable of delivering 2500 gallons per hour, and the two together could empty the travelling tank in about 1½ hours. Our picture shows the outer covering, which was arranged to provide a clear space of 3 in. between the covering and the tank itself, for free circulation of air for cooling purposes.

173 **Barry Railway, South Wales:** Mineral Train Brake Van.

The Barry Railway originated in the boom years of the nineteenth century, when the coal production of the South Wales valleys and the demand for such coal from overseas was to cause such congestion on the existing railways between the mines and the docks at Cardiff as to bring those railways almost to a standstill. The Barry Railway was built as an entirely new venture to connect a new port at Barry Island with the principal mining valleys. This handsome van was one of a series built by the Ashbury Railway Carriage and Wagon Company of Openshaw, Manchester, specially for the coal trains. It is in every way a period piece in wagon construction, in that no metal was used for the basic structure. The underframing was of the best selected Burmese teak, the body framing was of North American white oak, while the roof, doors, and end screens were of yellow pine. The side doors were framed in oak, and the roof boards were of yellow pine. The wheels had wrought-iron spokes, and from the original specification it was to be seen that the only steel items were the wheel-tyres and the axles. They were beautifully finished, and a fully detailed scale model of one of them today would make a most elegant ornament.

174 **Lynton and Barnstaple Railway:** Open-bogie Goods Wagon.

Reference has been made, under Plate 25, to the locomotive stock of this picturesque little 2 ft. gauge railway in north Devon. The passenger and goods rolling-stock, all brand new at the time of the opening in 1898 was equally distinguished. For passenger workings there were seventeen bogie coaches, and the original goods rolling-stock consisted of a total of twenty-four miscellaneous vehicles—some bogie, like the one illustrated, and others four-wheelers. They were all built by the Bristol Carriage and Wagon Company. In two respects they were in advance of much of the main line stock of the period. All vehicles passenger and goods alike were fitted with the vacuum automatic brake and centre-couplings. There were also side chains, used as an additional safety precaution. But another remarkable feature for the period was the use of roller-bearing axleboxes, though these were to some extent an experimental design and gave a lot of trouble. The equipping of all vehicles with the vacuum brake meant that goods wagons could be run in passenger trains as required, and in fact there were practically no goods trains as such—most of the regular passenger trains included an assortment of goods stock.

175 **Caledonian Railway:** McIntosh 4-6-0 Express Passenger Engine No. 50.

The success of the famous 'Dunalastair' series of 4-4-0 engines, and their exceptional capacity for handling heavy trains at high average speeds, did not entirely keep pace with the rapidly increasing weight of the principal expresses between

London and Glasgow, which by the years 1901-2 were being augmented by luxurious corridor carriages and by dining- and sleeping-cars. McIntosh therefore built, as an experiment, two very large engines, which could be described as a 4-6-0 version of the 'Dunalastair', with boilers that were among the largest in Great Britain at that time, feeding two cylinders 21 in. diameter by 26 in. stroke. These features, combined with the high working pressure of 200 lb. per sq. in., made the new engines, Nos. 49 and 50, the most powerful in the country at that time. The main consideration in their design was to work trains of 300 tons, unassisted, up the Beattock Bank, ten miles almost continuously on a gradient of 1 in 75. Despite their great power the outward appearance of these engines was quite exceptionally neat, and free from external gadgets, while the finish was in the traditional style of the Caledonian Railway. These engines certainly fulfilled their function, but it was not long before loads had increased to nearer 400 tons, and with such trains, rear-end banking assistance has to be provided at Beattock.

176 **Jura–Simplon Railway, Switzerland:** Express Passenger 4-6-0.

The one-time Jura–Simplon Railway provided one of the most important north to south routes through Switzerland for international traffic, and in addition to a considerable network in the north it included the fast running main line beside the Lake of Geneva and up the Rhône Valley to Brigue. In readiness for the opening of the Simplon Tunnel and the inauguration of a new through route to Italy, the powerful new four-cylinder compound 4-6-0s were introduced towards the end of 1902. They were built in the de Glehn style, with high pressure cylinders outside and low pressure inside; the diameters were 14 and $22\frac{1}{2}$ in. respectively, with a common stroke of 26 in. The engines were unusual in having Walschaerts valve gear for the outside cylinders and Joy's radial gear inside. The latter had the attraction of saving space by needing no eccentrics. The valve gears were thus a combination of Belgian and British design. The coupled wheels were 5 ft. 10 in. diameter and the boiler had a total of 1817 sq. ft. of heating surface. An interesting accessory is the device on the side of the tender indicating the water level, though this, of course, could not be read from the footplate. Presumably it was used as a guide to the firemen when filling the tank at intermediate stations.

177 **Minho-Douro Railway, Portugal:** 0-6-2 Tender Engine.

The Portuguese railways include an intriguing mixture of broad and narrow gauge lines now all under State management. The broad gauge lines are laid to a gauge that is a shade under 5 ft. 6 in. and operate mostly in the more level country in the south. A great many of the steam locomotives, for both broad and narrow gauge lines, were purchased from England, but the engine chosen for illustration, though characteristically British in all its externals, was actually built in Germany by the Hanover Locomotive Works at Linden. Use of the 0-6-2 wheel arrangement is unusual in a tender engine, particularly as there would appear to have been a considerable concentration of weight at the front end. The date of construction was 1902, and at that time it was no more than a moderately powered engine, with 18 in. by 26 in. cylinders, a total heating surface of 1575 sq. ft., and a grate area of only $21\frac{1}{2}$ sq. ft. To ensure a supply of dry sand, the sandbox was placed on top of the boiler as in American practice. Although no very fast running was contemplated, a speed recorder was included in the equipment, driven off the trailing end of the connecting-rod. The engine alone, without tender, weighed 47¾ tons.

178 **North Eastern Railway:** Express Passenger 4-6-0 Class 'S1'.

At the turn of the century very much heavier rolling-stock was being introduced on the Anglo-Scottish expresses over the East Coast route. The Great Northern Railway had already introduced the 'Atlantic' type of engine in 1898 (see ref. 99) but the first North Eastern move towards larger engines than the 4-4-0 lay in the 4-6-0 type, introduced by Wilson Wordsell in 1899, and the large variety that is the subject of our picture was built at Gateshead works in 1900. It was a huge engine for the period, but a most graceful design, with careful attention given to the general styling. It can be compared critically, for outward appearance, with the Caledonian engine of 1903 with which it could also be compared in tractive power. The North Easterns were free runners, and frequently attained maximum speeds of between 75 and 80 m.p.h. Their life on the principal express train services was relatively short because in 1903 Wilson Worsdell decided to adopt the Atlantic, rather than the 4-6-0 type for the most important duties (see ref. 105) This was in conformity with the North Eastern's partner in the East Coast service, the Great Northern which had standardized the Atlantic. Although short-lived on the main line, the North Eastern 'S1' 4-6-0 class was an important and handsome landmark in locomotive development.

179 **Wabash Railroad, U.S.A.:** Open Vestibuled Car.

This illustration provides a typical example of the kind of carriage that was coming into general use on the American railways in the early 1900s. It was of the open saloon type with centre vestibule, and at that time it is evident that smokers were in the minority. Seating was provided for sixty-six passengers and there was a small additional compartment to which persons who wished to smoke had to retire. The general external appearance of the car was typical of those being introduced on many railways, and was a product of the American Car and Foundry of St Louis. The particular car illustrated was gas lighted. Although American carriages were so large and so heavy, and in general rode well when they were on the run, there was a characteristic of railway travel in the U.S.A. that was not so pleasant. The buck-eye type of centre-coupler was used, and all too frequently some of these did connect while leaving a small amount of slack. When the powerful locomotive started up a long train one slack coupling could lead to the most severe jerks, and one who experienced this described the sensation as 'feeling as if one's neck was broken at every start'! In common with all American railways the Wabash used the Westinghouse type of continuous automatic brake.

180 **Cheshire Lines Committee:** Twelve-wheeled Composite Bogie Carriage.

The Cheshire Lines Committee was a joint concern of the Great Central, Great Northern, and Midland railways, and owned a busy network of lines based upon a fast main line between Liverpool and Manchester. Many of the trains conveyed through portions from Liverpool to destinations on one or another of the parent companies east of Manchester, and a good service was provided to Southport in strong competition with the Lancashire and Yorkshire Railway. For purely local working T. Parker, Locomotive Superintendent of the Great Central Railway, built some magnificent non-corridor twelve-wheelers, as illustrated, providing seating accommodation for seventeen first-class passengers and thirty-eight third class. They were finished in the varnished teak style used by both the Great Central and the Great Northern, though the style of coach, as would be expected from the designer, was in the Great Central fashion. They were lavishly finished in the somewhat overwhelming grandeur of the period, with woodwork in polished Spanish mahogany, with roofs and upper panels in Lincrusta Walton decorated with gold and colour. They were electrically lit, and the robust design of six-wheeled bogie provided very smooth riding.

181 **South Indian Railway:** Bogie Composite Carriage.

Indian railway carriages of the nineteenth century presented an unusual sight to European travellers in the sun-shades built out over the upper part of the bodies. These extensions afforded a primitive but effective way of keeping out the direct rays of the sun, and they were usually carried so far down that passengers would have to 'duck' under these awnings in order to enter the compartments. A great number of passengers were illiterate and so the classes were distinguished by colours. The shades varied somewhat on the various railways, though the basic colours were the same, so as to be understood throughout India. In these composite carriages the 'thirds' were often reserved for travellers' servants, and a communicating door was provided between the 'third' and the adjacent 'first'. In the South Indian coach illustrated, the third-class compartment immediately adjacent to the 'first' is actually labelled 'servants'. The South Indian Railway was one of those constructed on the metre gauge. The coaches themselves were built in India at the Negapatam Works of the company. The South Indian was one of the last in India to remain company-rather than State-owned.

182 **Dublin, Wicklow and Wexford Railway:** Restaurant Car for the Waterford Mail.

This line, which with certain absorptions in the south later became the Dublin and South Eastern Railway, provided the Irish end of the famous 'Irish Mail' route between London and Dublin. Kingstown, now Dun Laoghaire, was the Irish packet station, but in addition to the ordinary mail connection into Dublin there was an attractive mail train that went the opposite way. Leaving Dublin at 6.20 a.m. it reached Kingstown in time to connect with the arrival of the steamer from Holyhead, and then made its way southwards through to Wicklow and Wexford, and finally reaching Waterford at 10.5 a.m. As an attraction to tourists using this route, and undoubtedly to compete with the rival Great Western mail service via New Milford, the Dublin, Wicklow and Wexford Railway turned the mail into a very attractive breakfast-car express, consisting of four bogie carriages including kitchen-car, two six-wheelers which were non-corridor, and a six-wheeled travelling post-office van with apparatus for picking up and setting down mail-bags. As will be seen from our illustration, the first-class breakfast-car was a very handsome vehicle. All the bogie coaches included in the train had clerestory roofs, but the six-wheelers had flat roofs. All these coaches were built at the company's works at Grand Canal Street, Dublin.

183 **Great Western Railway:** Experimental 2-6-0 Heavy Freight Engine ('Kruger').

At the end of the nineteenth century greater engine power was needed for the increasing mineral traffic, and although William Dean was still in the chair at Swindon the influence of his chief assistant, G. J. Churchward, was evident in the developments in boiler design that were in progress. Some of the experimental designs caused intense surprise among admirers of Great Western locomotives, who had been accustomed to the very handsome outlines of previous standard locomotives. The 2-6-0, illustrated, and its isolated predecessor of the 4-6-0 type were about the ugliest of all. There was a high raised Belpaire firebox, and a large combustion chamber ahead of it. Because of the great size of the boiler an additional rear-end support was provided in a cradle giving support at the combustion chamber. A very ugly form of sandbox took the form of a saddle resting on top of the boiler at the front end, and steps were provided up the side of the boiler to give access for refilling. There were nine engines of the variety illustrated in our picture, and although they worked on the heavy coal trains between South Wales and Swindon via the Severn Tunnel they were finished in the ornate passenger livery. They were not particularly successful in traffic but provided many useful lessons in the gradual evolution of modern locomotive practice at Swindon. They are also notable as being one of the very few British locomotives of the period that could be called really ugly.

184 **Lake Shore and Michigan Southern:** 2-6-2 Express Passenger Locomotive.

The 2-6-2 type had no more than a passing wave of popularity in the U.S.A., and it was not adopted generally as were the Atlantic and later the Pacific. The reason was to be found in a certain instability in riding at high speed. This was attributed to the shorter connecting-rods, as compared with engines having a leading bogie. Nevertheless the type had its attractions, and the one illustrated, which was specially designed for high-speed service, was more successful than most. The cylinders were $20\frac{1}{2}$ in. diameter by 28 in. stroke, and the coupled wheels 6 ft. 8 in. diameter. The boiler was a large one with a total heating surface of 3597 sq. ft., and the wide firebox had a grate area of $48\frac{1}{2}$ sq. ft. They were built by Brooks in 1901. They were sufficiently successful for a repeat order to be placed for more engines of the same design. The use of bar frames, as usual in American practice, and the high pitch of the boiler centre line frequently gave locomotives a spidery appearance; but these Lake Shore 2-6-2s with their big wheels had a grace all of their own. They were in any case representative of a very interesting phase in locomotive development. It is curious that Brooks also built some high-speed 4-6-0s for this same road in 1900, with an almost identical tractive effort. But the firebox had to be a narrow one, with 36.6 sq. ft. of grate area, and the boiler had a total heating surface of 2890 sq. ft. The change to the 2-6-2 type in 1901 was clearly made to permit of the use of a wide firebox and greater heating surface.

185 **Pennsylvania Railroad:** Class 'E1' Atlantic of 1899.

The Pennsylvania was one of the greatest of American railroads, and unlike most others built the majority of its locomotives in its own shops at Altoona. This great centre which included a stationary locomotive testing plant was described as the 'Crewe' of the U.S.A. At the end of the nineteenth century Theodore N. Ely was chief of motive power, and he had a very able mechanical designer in Alexander S. Vogt. It was during this fruitful partnership, in 1899, that the remarkable Atlantic engine shown in our picture was designed and built at Altoona. It was of the 'Mother Hubbard' type, and the 4-4-2 wheel arrangement was exploited to the utmost for providing a huge firebox. The cylinders were 20½ in. diameter by 26 in. stroke, and the coupled wheels 6 ft. 8 in. diameter. The total heating surface though large by contemporary British standards was no more than moderate in the U.S.A., namely 2320 sq. ft., but the firebox had a grate area of no less than 68 sq. ft.! How the fireman, working on the open platform at the rear, managed to keep such a grate covered is hard to imagine. The 'E1' class of 1899 was the pioneer in a notable development of the Atlantic type at Altoona. Even after the Pacific type had been introduced for the heaviest duties the Atlantic remained, for high-speed work, and the final design, the 'E6S' of 1915, with cylinders 23½ in. diameter by 26 in. stroke was one of the most powerful Atlantics ever built.

186 **Paris, Lyons and Mediterranean Railway:** 4-6-0 Mixed Traffic Locomotive.

The 'P.L.M.' was one of the largest of French railways prior to nationalization, and of its various standard types of locomotives there were large numbers of each. The small-wheeled 4-6-0 which is the subject of our picture was a 'maid of all work', taking express trains on the secondary routes, such as that from Belfort to Lyons, and doing a great deal of the work along the Côte d'Azur. The latter is a difficult route, with awkward grading, and continuous sharp curvature between Marseilles and Toulon, and where it follows the coast between St Raphael and the Italian frontier. These engines were in general use on that line until the early 1920s. In view of the moderate speeds involved one might question the need for the streamlined fairings between the chimney and dome, and in the conical front of the smokebox. In the region of the Rhône delta however the line is exposed to the effects of the Mistral—that tearing wind from the Alps than can carry all before it. There is no doubt that the 'streamlining' would noticeably reduce air resistance in such adverse weather, when the speed of the train in relation to the surrounding air currents could be much the same as that of a modern electric express travelling at nearly 100 m.p.h.

187–188 **French Railway Signals**

To anyone who travelled on the French railways at any time up to the year 1930 the signals would have presented objects of fascinating interest, yet in the absence of expert explanation, a perpetual mystery. The various companies all had their own pet practices. There was nothing remotely representing a national code, except in the general acceptance as an absolute stop signal of the red and white chess-board, or *carré*. When displayed as in our picture, the order to stop was as definite as that from the British home signal. There was nevertheless a fundamental difference in principle for in moving to the all-clear position the *carré* pivoted about a vertical centre line to be seen edge-on; in other words it became virtually invisible. The French accepted that no signal at all could be taken as all-clear; one proceeded, unless told to slow down, or stop. The green and white chess-board, and the red disc were adopted only by certain railways. The green and white board was used as a repeater of the next red and white board ahead on lines which used the red disc for the purpose later to be described. The green and white signal was something akin to an English distant, though it had no connection with the block working except on the Paris–Orléans Railway. The signal giving entrance to the next block section, on the majority of lines, was a semaphore, and the red disc was a repeater of the block semaphore. If a driver encountered a red disc in the position shown in our picture, and the other signals were edge-on it would be a warning to him to slow down and be prepared to stop at the semaphore giving entrance to the next block section. If the red and white *carré* was clear, but the green and white board facing, as shown, the driver would be advised to be ready to stop much sooner than the semaphore block signal, at a red and white *carré* no more than about 300 yds. ahead. It was one of the complications and contradictions of the old-time French signalling that the Paris–Orléans Railway used the green and white chess-board as a repeater for the semaphore block signal.

189 **London & South Western Railway:** Dugald Drummond's Four-cylinder 4-6-0 Mixed Traffic Engine.

In 1905 there seemed to be a competition among British locomotive engineers as to who could build the largest and most powerful locomotive. The Caledonian 4-6-0, reference 175 was a strong claimant for this distinction, in 1903, but two years later that handsome engine was eclipsed by the L.S.W.R. giant illustrated, in sheer size and weight. It is significant however that in the heat of this competition the characteristic British elegance of outline was retained. Drummond intended these huge engines for express traffic, but they had a curious mixture of valve gear: Walschaerts for the outside cylinders and Stephenson's for the inside, and despite their very impressive appearance they proved somewhat sluggish in traffic. On a line when a free-running engine was essential for maintaining the fast schedules these engines proved comparative failures, and they were relegated to fast goods work, in which they put in many years of hard revenue-earning service. Although they did not fulfil their original object the design was a landmark in locomotive development, in the production of a very large, free-steaming boiler, and an object lesson in handsome styling.

190 **Eastern Railway of France:** Four-cylinder Compound 4-6-0 Locomotive.

Elsewhere in this book it has been told how the de Glehn compound system was developed in France to great advantage in the Atlantic engines of the Northern and Paris–Orleans railways. The Eastern used the Atlantic type to no more than an experimental extent, and made the 4-6-0 its principal express type from the early years of the twentieth century; this was quickly developed to produce the remarkable superheated version shown in our picture. So far as the continent of Europe is concerned this engine is in some ways a postscript to our period and a portent of things to come. It was one of the earliest examples of a locomotive in which compounding and superheating were combined. For many years the two principles were usually considered as *alternatives*, rather than allies towards the increasing of efficiency in locomotives. The photograph on which our picture was based was taken at La Villette, Paris, in 1934 when the engine concerned—one of a large class—was still in its original condition. Some of them were subsequently modernized, and for a few years did work that was equivalent of that regularly performed by Pacifics. As originally built the cylinder diameters were 15¼ in. high pressure, and 23⅖ in. low pressure, both sets with a stroke of 26¾ in. The boiler was a large one with a total heating surface of more than 2000 sq. ft. and a grate area of 34 sq. ft. The coupled wheels were 6 ft. 10 in. diameter, and the engines were capable of hauling 300-ton trains up gradients of 1 in 200 at 60 m.p.h.

191 **A Russian 0-8-0 Shunting Tank Engine.**

This locomotive is one of the very few illustrated in this book that were not supplied to a public railway system. It was engaged in industrial service for the Russian Iron and Coal Industry Co. Ltd., but it includes a number of interesting features, not least in the evidence of British influence in a locomotive built by a German firm for Russian industry in 1903. It ran on the Russian standard main line gauge of 5 ft. To enable sharp curves to be negotiated the wheel-base was made as short as possible, and the eight-coupled wheels, of 3 ft. 11½ in. grouped close together, with considerable resulting overhang front and rear. The two cylinders were 18⅛ in. diameter by 24¾ in. stroke. Slide valves were used, actuated by the English-designed Joy valve gear. At one time this was very popular in Russia, and in keeping with Continental ideas on accessibility, the valve gear was outside—the jack-link connection to the connecting-rod being prominent. As the engine was engaged entirely in industrial use continuous brakes were not fitted, and in fact brakes were applied only to the leading and trailing coupled wheels. The boiler had a total heating surface of 1206 sq. ft. and a grate area of 23¾ sq. ft. The engine is shown in the livery then standard on the Russian State Railways.

192 **Gothard Railway:** 0-8-0 Heavy Freight Locomotive.

It is perhaps appropriate to end with this fine locomotive for the Gothard line is one of the most spectacular in the world. Originally an independent company it was acquired by the State early in the present century, and incorporated organizationally in the Swiss Federal Railway system in 1908. The outstanding physical characteristics are, of course, the northern and southern 'ramps', as the great inclines leading to the Gothard Tunnel are known. On these the gradients are 1 in 37 for many miles, leading through countless tunnels, and round the famous spirals in the neighbourhood of Wassen and Giornico. In contrast to some of the complicated compound engines used on many Continental railways this Gothard 0-8-0 is a two-cylinder simple, but one of great power. The cylinders were 20½ in. diameter by 24 in. stroke, coupled wheels 3 ft. 9 in. diameter, and the large boiler, the size of which is somewhat dwarfed by its low centre-line, has a total heating surface of 1757 sq. ft., and a grate area of 23 sq. ft. The whole design is one of great simplicity, including the use of Stephenson's link motion, instead of the more usual Walschaerts gear. The former is, of course, ideal for a hard-slogging mountain goods engine.

INDEX